TSODILO HILLS

TSODILO HILLS

Copper Bracelet of the Kalahari

Edited by Alec Campbell, Larry Robbins,
and Michael Taylor, with James G. Workman

Michigan State University Press • East Lansing
The Botswana Society • Gaborone

∞ The paper used in this publication meets the minimum requirements of
ANSI/NISO Z39.48–1992 (R 1997) (Permanence of Paper).

 Michigan State University Press

East Lansing, Michigan 48823–5245

 The Botswana Society

Gaborone, Botswana

Printed and bound in China.

18 17 16 15 14 13 12 11 10   1 2 3 4 5 6 7 8 9 10

Library of Congress Cataloging-in-Publication Data

Tsodilo hills : copper bracelet of the Kalahari / edited by Alec Campbell ... [et al.].

p. cm.

Includes bibliographical references and index.

ISBN 978-0-87013-858-4 (pbk. : alk. paper) 1. Tsodilo Hills (Botswana)—Antiquities. 2. Tsodilo Hills (Botswana)—Description and travel.

I. Campbell, Alec C., 1932-

DT2520.T76T76 2008

968.83—dc22

2008043929

Cover and book design by

The Creative Type

Cape Town, South Africa

Front cover:
Evening light on Tsodilo's Female Hill.

Inside front cover:
*In 1964, two Juc'hoan sit before the painted panel
to which Laurens van der Post gave his name.*

Frontispiece:
*Bichrome painting of cattle on west cliff of
Child Hill in shades of red superimposed on faded
geometric designs. There are about 160 paintings
of cattle, mostly on Female Hiill.*

Visit Michigan State University Press on the World Wide Web at: www.msupress.msu.edu

Visit The Botswana Society on the World Wide Web at: www.botswanabeckons.com

CONTENTS

ACKNOWLEDGMENTS

The Tsodilo Hills (Male and Female are really "mountains") began to form about six hundred million years ago and have been visited and periodically occupied by people for at least one hundred thousand years and probably for much longer.

Written records about the Hills commenced only in 1898 when Siegfried Passarge drew a sketch map of the Hills and wrote briefly about their geology and rock art. Sporadically, a very few others came to look, to note the archaeology, to hunt (one shot the last local rhinoceros in 1935), and to enjoy the sheer beauty of these amazing hills where wind whispers through the rocks messages we do not understand and the evening sun colors the cliffs with a copper glow. It was only in the late 1950s that Laurens van der Post brought the Hills to public attention with his book *The Lost World of the Kalahari*.

Map A.1 (right): The location of Tsodilo Hills in southern Africa.

Fig. A.1 (preceding page): Evening light causes long cliffs on Female Hill to glow like burnished copper giving the Hills one of their many names, "Copper Bracelet of the Evening."

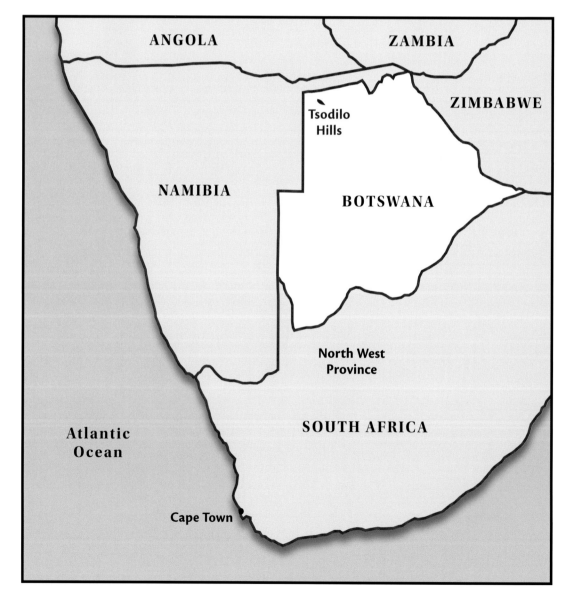

Alec Campbell first visited Tsodilo in 1963 with George Silberbauer, a highly respected ethnographer of the San in Botswana. One look at those amazing rock faces soaring above the desert captured his mind and heart, and he set out to record as much as he could of their history, their rock paintings, and the people who have intermittently inhabited them for a hundred millennia.

As Director of Botswana's National Museum, Campbell was backed by a little government finance to search the Hills, record the art, and excavate the ancient rock shelters. In 1982, he was joined at Depression Shelter by Larry Robbins, a professional archaeologist on a Fulbright Scholarship teaching at the University of Botswana. Over the following years, Robbins brought American students to help Campbell and National Museum staff to excavate White Paintings Shelter, Rhino Cave, Ancestors' Cave, and Kudu Horn Shelter. Chief among his students was Mike Murphy, who was to be awarded his doctorate on work done in White Paintings Shelter and who then participated at every successive site.

Campbell, Robbins, and Murphy, working as a team, were joined by George Brook, a paleo-geographer from Athens, Georgia, who dated dunes and paleo-lakes, excavations, and a cupule in Rhino Cave. This group located more than twenty prehistoric specularite and mica mines, dug test pits in some of them, and showed that the heyday of a long mining period peaked and then declined between about AD 850–1150. Adam Kiehn also worked on the mines. James Denbow, one-time senior archaeologist at the National Museum, and Edwin Wilmsen, American anthropologist and recorder of Western Ngamiland history, assisted by Tsau Xau, Hildi Hendrickson, Dean Jacobson, and Gillian Turner, and by museum staff, excavated the Iron Age villages of Divuyu and Nqoma and several small rock shelters. Wilmsen went on to excavate Later Stone Age and Iron Age artifacts in Ta'shra (Dancing Penises) Shelter. Denbow and Wilmsen were assisted in their research by Gcau C'untae, Tcashe C'untae, Tchise Gcau, and Shoroka Tchishe (also known as Shoroka Gcau), all from Tsodilo, and by Tsao K'ao, Dam Qam, Qam Tcishe, and John Marengo, from the Caecae area. In South Africa, Duncan Miller analyzed the metal artifacts from the village sites.

During the 1990s, the National Museum staff with Campbell and funded by Sweden through the Folkens Museum, Stockholm, recorded some four hundred rock-paintings sites and over four thousand individual paintings. Nick Walker, then senior curator of archaeology at the National Museum, excavated at Corner Cave and other shelters, being mainly interested in rock cupules and grooves. Michael Taylor, Assistant Curator of Ethnology at the Museum, developed an interest in Tsodilo, having heard about it from his father, an amateur archaeologist, who had organized an archaeological expedition from the University of Cape Town to Tsodilo in 1964. Michael collected histories, genealogies, and social relations of late-nineteenth- and twentieth-century Hambukushu and San peoples at Tsodilo, which later linked to his doctoral thesis. Bob Hitchcock independently collected information on modern San and their art in Western Botswana, particularly from administrators at Kuru Development Trust at D'kar, including Braam and Willemien LeRoux and Maudi Brown, who explored with a number of San artists the essentials of painting and printing techniques, and from the artists themselves.

All this research resulted in numerous papers and articles published mainly in scientific journals. Little research would have been possible without funding by outside foundations and enormous help from museum staff, students, and friends. In 2001, the main authors determined to collect research results together, to adjust the language to make it more reader friendly, and to publish it so that nonscientists would also have the opportunity to read and learn about these amazing Hills.

It is impossible to name all those who have helped with research over the last forty-five years. We thank George Silberbauer, who first took Alec Campbell to Tsodilo; without that visit, this book might never have been written.

The Office of the President issued research permits, and successive directors of the National Museum—Doreen Nteta, Tarisayi Madondo, Tjako Mpulubusi, and Tickey Pule—made research possible. John Gould and the late Alan Simpkin, Department of Surveys and Lands, provided much-needed help with mechanical knowledge and mapping. The National Science Foundation, the National Geographic Society, the Wenner-

Gren Foundation, the American Embassy in Botswana, Botswana Life Insurance Limited, and Michigan State University all made grants of various amounts.

Many employees of the National Museum assisted in excavations and searched for rock art sites and prehistoric mines. To name just a few, Lopang Tatlhego, who crawled through mine tunnels no larger than his body; the late Alex Matseka, who took part in almost every excavation until his tragic death; Otukile Ralegoreng, a National Museum driver who discovered Rhino Cave; and Grace Babutsi, who helped sink the seven-meter hole in White Paintings Shelter. Stefan Strand, Jimmy Mashonja, Calvin Sebole, Gordon Metz, Mogogi Ledimo, the late Leonard Ramotokwane, Salalenna Greek Phaladi, Nonofho Mathibidi, Doreen Nteta, and Tjako Mpulubusi were all also involved in excavations or in the search for and recording of rock art sites.

Robbins brought students Dennis Cherry and Troy Ferone to work at White Paintings Shelter. Brook brought Andrew Ivester, who wrote a master's thesis on the sediments of White Paintings Shelter. Many of our friends excavated, sorted "dirt," and helped in camp—Jeremy Clark, Julian Harris, Mike Main, Richard and Marian Hartland-Rowe, Ralph Raubenheimer, Wright Kgosietsile, and John Hardy, who discovered the "Elephant Panel," all took part.

Our wives and children also worked at Tsodilo. George Brook's son, Duncan, discovered Ancestors' Cave, Niall Campbell acted as interpreter, while Colin and Heather Campbell walked the Hills in search of paintings. Judy Campbell helped cook and undertook much of the washing up. Lark Murphy excavated at White Paintings Shelter. Pat Robbins and children Dan, Michael, and Mark also all worked one season excavating. Katrin Taylor kept Michael smiling and sane through many dusty days and nights in the sandveld of Ngamiland, as he documented the stories and memories of absolute heroes and heroines whose encyclopedic knowledge exposed an astounding richness of heritage and history. Janet Brashler excavated at White Paintings Shelter and, after leaving, sent us much-needed food and drinks. Bob Hitchcock and Mike Bryan were among the first to help record rock art. Anne Murray of the Ethnographic Museum in Stockholm made possible the major rock art recording program, during which Joe Alphers taught National Museum staff, including Bonolo Lekula and Abram Magowe, how to photograph rock paintings for permanent record purposes.

In Botswana, Bernard Vink analyzed specularite and mica schist and Bill Downey obtained luminescence dates on sand excavated in shelters. In the United States and Canada, Alison Brooks, James Feathers, and Bob Kalin, respectively, obtained dates on ostrich eggshell, sand, and laterite. Beverly Smith provided an initial sorting of the fauna. Kathlyn Stewart identified fish bones. Richard Klein and Richard Milo analyzed mammal bones. Nancy Jeanne Stevens and the late J. Alan Holman identified reptiles. Chris Appleton identified shellfish from the ancient lake and Kurt Haberyan studied diatoms. In South Africa, Judy Sealy obtained a date on a sheep bone excavated in White Paintings Shelter. Randolph Donahue studied use-wear on stone tools from both Depression and White Paintings Shelters. We thank Megan Biesele for information on the mythology attached to the Tsodilo Hills, and Nick Walker for help with excavations, for recording the art, and particularly for sharing his work on cupules and grooves.

The late Kabo Mosweu introduced Bob Hitchcock to the world of San music and art. Hitchcock's artist informants at Kuru included the late Coexae Gqam (also known as Dada), Coexae Bob, Ngcabe Taase (also known as Nxabe), Gcose Ntoxo, Xaga, Thamae Setshogo (also known as Tamai), Thamae Kaashe, Sobe Sobe, Qaetcao Moses (also known as Olebogeng), Gxaoco Xare, Gxaiga Qhomanca, Gamnxoa, Qoexoa, and Gqam. Other informants included Qwaa (also known as Mangana or Geelboi), Mieke van der Post, and Mathias Guenther.

David Coulson of the Trust for African Rock Art (TARA), Nairobi, author and photographer, gave us free use of his magnificent collection of rock art slides taken at Tsodilo. Rowena White and Reuben Chelimo, also of TARA, cleaned, scanned, and color corrected numerous slides.

Most important of all were the residents of the two villages at Tsodilo, Hambukushu and Juc'hoansi, who assisted us over more than forty years. We greatly appreciate the help of the late Benjamin Dihama, Campbell's first

Fig. A.2 (above):
Baobab growing on gently sloping windblown sand below the cliffs of Female Hill.
Baobabs occur mainly on the west side of the Hills.

guide to rock art sites. We thank Gcau, Xauwe, Ronson, and Shoroka, sadly now all passed on, who acted as guides, informants, and friends over many years. They showed us the Sex Site, the ritual site Ncaekhoe still used in the mid-nineteenth century, and the place where God lowered from heaven the first animals and people onto the Hills.

For forty-five years, Samutjau Mukate, Headman at Tsodilo, looked after us, shared water from his well, and acted as guide, excavator, and informant. As time passed and western influences in Tsodilo increased, Samutjau recognized that his people's cultural history was disappearing and, fearful it would be lost with his death, revealed secrets of Tsodilo, asking that they be recorded for posterity. MmaMukate, Samutjau's wife, sang for us the song used in curing "madness" and fed us quantities of *mogwana*, a mildly alcoholic drink made from grewia berries.

After we had collected together and rewritten in a single manuscript our scientific papers and those scraps of information that bind them together, we asked James Workman, American writer and journalist, to rewrite the manuscript in a form suitable for general reading. We thank Janet Hermans for support during final publication negotiations and Neil Parsons and Derek Jones of the Botswana Society.

We are very grateful indeed to Sally Owen and Catherine Guest of The Creative Type, Cape Town, who visited Tsodilo and were so impressed by the Hills, the art, and the people that they undertook the layout of this book at an absolute minimal cost. We thank Norman and Nell Hardy for providing funds to support editing and Rupert and Clare McCammon, who covered all the costs of scanning and color correcting the numerous illustrations. Marieka Brouwer scanned the map. Special thanks are due to Julie Loehr and Kristine Blakeslee of MSU Press for their help in shepherding this book along on its way to publication.

Finally, the editors thank their families profusely for their encouragement and support for the long journey that has led to the production of this book. ∎

Approaching the Heart
of the Kalahari

Alec Campbell,
Larry Robbins, and
Michael Taylor

INTRODUCTION

You approach Tsodilo Hills in one of several ways. The first and oldest, of course, is by foot. For more than one hundred millennia people came across the Kalahari's gently rolling, tree-covered dunes to arrive at the increasingly sacred place: an unexpected and rocky enigma, rising precipitously out of a sea of sand.

These people remained largely interdependent upon each other and upon the land and its resources. They came to hunt, to gather, to drink water, to celebrate, to dwell, to mine, to trade, to dance, to heal, to mourn. Later, they departed on foot, leaving behind accidental evidence of their visits to and sojourns in the Hills.

The second approach is by vehicle or airplane. The last century has witnessed an increasing flow of humans arriving by this method from ever-more-distant origins. By recent count, ten thousand people a year journey by four-wheel-drive. These seekers have become largely self-contained, independent. They navigate by map and satellite positioning rather than by memory or stars. They arrive swiftly, over the course of mere hours, rolling over the sand waves until they, too, stop, cut the engine, and emerge from the cooling vehicle. Then even they must make the final approach on foot, looking up, to the Hills.

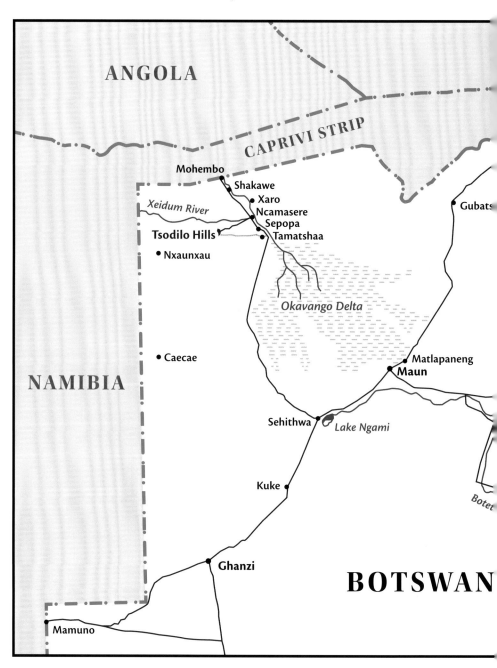

Fig. 0.1 (preceding page):
The road crossing the sand ridge west of Gubekho Gorge. The Reception Center and Site Museum lie just beyond the baobab tree, while Male Hill in the background towers four hundred meters above the plain.

Map 0.1 (right):
The location of Tsodilo Hills in Botswana.

Copper Bracelet of the Kalahari

An Ice Age has passed between the first and the most recent arrivals. Yet little has diminished the majestic, brooding quality of their fixed destination. The first glimpse of Tsodilo can inspire awe even among the jaded. The western cliffs of the Hills radiate a strange light, light that in the copper glow of sunset becomes an incandescent beacon that can be seen for miles across the rolling landscape. Of the many names that Tsodilo has undoubtedly gained over the millennia, few can be as evocative as the Juc'hoansi name derived from its sunset glow: "Copper Bracelet of the Evening," or more simply Tqxi nqum, "Copper Hills."

Modern arrivals also bring to Tsodilo the most advanced tools of their day. They use this equipment to gather "roots" of a different sort, and to hunt elusive quarry: clues to human history. The answers they find only give rise to deeper questions: Where does Tsodilo's energy come from? Why have the Hills felt so alive to so many for so long? What is it about this place that draws humans to it like iron filings to a colossal magnet?

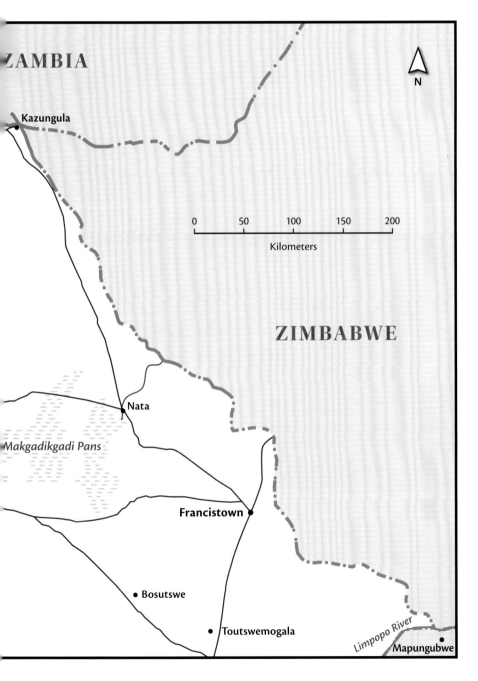

It is not, after all, the biggest geological rock formation in Africa. Nor is it the highest mountain, the most prominent plateau, the most jagged range, or the most precipitous cliff. It is not even the oldest stone on earth's most ancient continent. Lacking these easy and obvious superlatives, Tsodilo has been largely neglected by the age of explorers, geographers, and modern travel agent brochures as little more than a place of rock art, but this is rapidly changing with the dawn of a new century. Tsodilo will never be merely a box to be ticked by been-there-done-that mass-market tourism; there are no urban centers nearby, no noisy resorts or shopping malls.

Yet those seekers who are prepared to gain a more complex and layered insight into Africa will come, as they always have. Those who open themselves to surprises will continue to delight in each new facet the Hills open to them. They will, invariably, depart with questions. For too long there has been an awkward and sometimes painful chasm of incomprehension between those who have come on foot and those who arrive on four wheels. This book will not close the gap. It merely makes the first real collaborative attempt by the latter visitors to build a bridge strong

enough for all parties to journey across, look back, and gain perspective on the place from which they have come. It offers, perhaps, a third way to approach Tsodilo—through understanding.

Rosetta Stone of the Kalahari

The first outsiders, typically European, saw Tsodilo as an African "curiosity," a stone canvas decorated by "Bushmen." Some romanticized the place wonderfully as an outdoor museum on par with those in Europe. Others publicized it, celebrated it, made up stories about it. Yet all the while its value seemed static, cold, and two-dimensional: rock paintings of a bygone era by people frozen in time.

Only in recent decades has a more profound, nuanced, and living interpretation begun to materialize. To be sure, it remains one of the most extraordinary sites of remote prehistoric art in southern Africa. Here more than four thousand individual paintings from over four hundred sites have been systematically surveyed, catalogued, and recorded on film. The paintings are a feast for the eyes. Yet to focus so narrowly and exclusively on Tsodilo's art is to obscure the dynamic reality that is now emerging.

The Hills have slowly revealed many of their secrets to the trowels and sieves of archaeologists, secrets that had been hidden, sealed by the windblown sands of time. Brought to the light, they fuse the two-dimensional rock art with the larger setting, connecting time and geography across the subcontinent. They indicate that, far beyond merely being Laurens van der Post's "Louvre of the Kalahari," the Tsodilo Hills can perhaps be seen as a cross-cultural, multidimensional "Rosetta Stone" of the Kalahari, covered in enigmatic art. Now specialists are decoding their data to help unlock questions of human origins through a complexity of layers—trade, tools, metalworking, fishing, agriculture, animal husbandry, hunting, sexuality, interaction, art, spirituality, status slowly clarifying the past, while bringing relevance to the present.

This more significant profile did not just emerge at once, through a single insight. It has been accumulating steadily through a progression of stages. Instead of working in isolation, Tsodilo scholars began to share and connect the findings from their separate disciplines, weaving together a more integrated whole. They teamed up, established linkages between discoveries, and began connecting: livestock to art; art to age; age to geology; geology to climate; climate to resources; resources to economies; economies to trade; trade to values; values to art.

The nature and implications of these discoveries and linkages are detailed in the following chapters. Yet a sampling of five breakthroughs by researchers of this place suggests that our conventional wisdom about Tsodilo and its inhabitants may need radical updating. Results of archaeological excavations have changed the interpretations of the past human record in the Kalahari in fundamental ways.

Provocative New Interpretations

First, consider occupation. The Kalahari has often been referred to as an "empty" part of southern Africa that was occupied only as hunting and gathering people sought refuge in the area from more powerful groups migrating into the fertile areas of southern Africa. At best, it was assumed that the Kalahari was an archaeological backwater that had little to offer. The most important archaeological sites were found in other areas, especially in South Africa and Zimbabwe, while the Kalahari was little known. However, in the early 1980s and 1990s four archaeologists uncovered a wealth of Middle Stone Age materials at Tsodilo, including beautifully worked small stone points, which must have been mounted as spears or some perhaps even as arrowheads **(figs. 3.11 & 3.19)**. These most probably dated back more than sixty thousand years. The earliest remains from White Paintings Shelter, excavated just above bedrock at a depth of seven meters, pushed human occupation back to at least one hundred thousand years ago. Archaeologists also have uncovered a great richness of Later Stone Age tools, along with evidence of one of the most continuous records of the use of beads known anywhere.

Fig. 0.3 (above):

The Elephant Panel. The right half of this 20-meter-long panel is hidden behind foliage. A second faded and now almost invisible large elephant stands above the elephant at the left. To the right are images of two leather bags, a cow facing left, an antelope facing right standing beside a small elephant, more faded antelope and human figures. Note the line drawn from the cow that loops down under the small elephant and rises to the head of an antelope facing left. Below this line are images of possible root plants above a further badly eroded huge elephant. Below the large elephant at the left is a man with penis facing right above a geometric design with short horizontal bars. A somewhat similar geometric rock painting occurs at Manyana Village in southeastern Botswana.

Next, there's mining. In 1991, after a difficult climb on Female Hill, a group of archaeologists came across a magnificent painted panel featuring a red elephant **(fig. 0.3)**. While the others admired the painting, one of the archaeologists, Mike Murphy, began exploring a naturally concealed narrow valley nearby. In it he found a cave.

Their curiosity aroused, the archaeologists began excavating and realized that the cave was, in fact, a mine, with a mound of debris, or tailings, located in front of the entrance. This was unprecedented and they continued to search elsewhere at Tsodilo. Eventually they located more than twenty mines and excavated in many of them to see what the ancient miners sought. The main ore proved to be specularite, a glittering iron derivative; but mica schist, another glittering substance, and quartz were also mined. Mining at Tsodilo began centuries before the rise of such important sites as Great Zimbabwe.

Third, hunting and gathering were long held to be the primary, if not exclusive, economies practiced by the arid region's earliest inhabitants. This is a somewhat romantic idea. It perpetuates a belief that there are "correct" and "progressive" stages of societal development and that the aboriginal populations lived in splended isolation, a lifestyle that saw little, if any, contact or change through the millennia. In this view the Kalahari Desert was a formidable barrier, marginal to the main events in African prehistory.

That image began to change, starting in the 1980s, when two researchers working under the auspices of the National Museum of Botswana excavated the remains of the sixth- to eleventh-century settlements now called Divuyu and Nqoma. The early inhabitants were village farming peoples who raised goats and cattle, grew crops, and were involved—based on the evidence left behind—in long-distance trade. The families here not only grew their own subsistence food; they also may have traded their surplus cattle and specularite for smelted copper and iron, for seashells from the Atlantic and Indian Oceans, and for glass beads from the Middle East. All this evidence working together has begun to create a new picture that clearly reveals that the inhabitants were anything but isolated. Indeed, Tsodilo is being gradually elevated into its proper place as a pivotal center for first-millennium trade, despite being located in the middle of the dry Kalahari Desert.

That brings up a fourth field for revision. Was it always so dry and inhospitable here? The question leads us to another exciting finding about Tsodilo's distant past: the unexpected discovery of wetland environments and a long record of fishing. The Tsodilo Hills once bordered an ancient and now extinct lake. The longest record of freshwater fish exploitation in southern Africa was uncovered at White Paintings Shelter. Hundreds of fish bones, some dated to over thirty thousand years, bear witness to systematic exploitation of spawning runs of large catfish and bream. Whether the fish were caught in the ancient lake or from the Ncamasere River north of the Hills remains uncertain, but the possibility of fishing directly at Tsodilo may be confirmed. The skillfully carved barbed bone harpoon or spear points (**fig. 3.7**) found at Tsodilo that were used to obtain fish during certain periods had not previously been found at any archaeological sites in southern Africa. The nearest similar finds were located more than 1,500 kilometers away at sites in the eastern part of Democratic Republic of Congo and along the ancient beaches of Lake Turkana in Kenya. Such finds are also evident along the Nile, as well as in the Sahara. Indeed, the evidence of intensive fish consumption in the currently dry environment of Tsodilo was a remarkable find because today the closest fish swim in the Okavango River, separated from the Hills by 50 kilometers of dune fields. However, an ancient lake at Tsodilo and the Ncamasere River, which flowed until modern times 16 kilometers north of the Hills, may have been sources of the fish.

The final stories have come less from what the Hills reveal about their former inhabitants than from what the current inhabitants reveal about the Hills. By respectfully engaging their voices and memories, we better appreciate what Tsodilo means to past and present, and can fill in some of the links that archaeology left vacant.

Tsodilo is, uniquely, the only concentration of rock art in southern Africa still inhabited by San people. It is the ancestors of the Khoe and San who are believed to have been responsible for creating much of the rock art of southern Africa, including the great majority of paintings at Tsodilo. The remembered and recorded history of these peoples over the past two centuries offer a fascinating insight into the wider dynamics of power between the different peoples inhabiting the region we now call Ngamiland. Khoesan lived alongside Bantu-speakers around the Okavango for centuries as equals. However, this began to change in the early 1800s. At that time the Batawana began forming a powerful centralized kingdom on the edge of the Okavango Delta, subjugating the Khoesan into servitude and taking over their land, as had happened elsewhere in the subcontinent. Over the course of a century,

Fig. 0.5 (above):
Gcau C'untae was the "elder statesman" of the Juc'hoansi before he passed away at the age of about eighty. With his passing, an encyclopedia of knowledge on the Hills and their environs was lost. Some of his knowledge had been shared with younger generations in his village, but in these times of great social change, many younger villagers are less interested in their history. Sadly, researchers only documented a minute fraction of what he knew.

Fig. 0.4 (left):
Samutjau Mukate (in 1988), Headman of Tsodilo village, diviner, herbalist, raconteur of local history and once skilled blacksmith. He holds the two sticks that operate a pair of small bellows still used by Hambukushu and Wayeyi to heat charcoal for working iron.

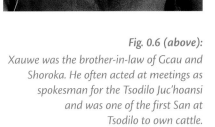

Fig. 0.6 (above):
Xauwe was the brother-in-law of Gcau and Shoroka. He often acted at meetings as spokesman for the Tsodilo Juc'hoansi and was one of the first San at Tsodilo to own cattle.

Fig. 0.7 (left):
Shoroka, Gcau's younger brother and also deceased, was renowned as a storyteller among the Juc'hoansi.

Fig. 0.8 (above):
C'untae Gcau, son of Gcau C'untae, Headman of the Juc'hoansi village at Tsodilo.
(Like Hambukushu, the eldest son in Juc'hoansi society takes his father's names in reverse order.)

the San in Ngamiland were almost completely subjugated, with one exception: Tsodilo. Tsodilo earned a place in the midst of this history as one of the last outposts of undisputed Khoesan ownership, an area that its Khoesan "owners" were able to protect as their own until finally capitulating at the beginning of the twentieth century.

Tsodilo today has two permanent settlements, Hambukushu and Juc'hoansi. The two extended families, whose clusters of homes are separated by a couple of kilometers, have a long history of association with one another, with the Hills and, more recently, with the research that has been conducted at Tsodilo. They have acted as guides, assisted in archaeological excavations, and shared their extensive knowledge of the Hills and their history. It is in large part due to them, particularly Samutjau Mukate, leader of the Hambukushu (fig. 0.4), and the late Gcau C'untae, leader of the Juc'hoansi village (fig. 0.5), that the stories in this book can be told.

Tsodilo Belongs to the World

This book owes its stories to the people who have shared them with its authors over the last three decades. Yet the stories of Tsodilo belong not just to them, or even to the nation of Botswana; they belong to the world. In recognition of the broader value of the Tsodilo Hills to local, national, and global heritage, an early management plan was established by the National Museum in 1994. Funds allowed for the National Museum Headquarters, with its site museum, boreholes for water, housing, and tourist facilities. In 2001, the complex was opened by His Excellency, President Festus Mogae, and application was made to United Nations Environmental, Scientific and Cultural Organisation (UNESCO) to have the Hills declared a "World Heritage Site," a status that was granted the very next year. Further background to the granting of World Heritage status is given by Phillip Segadika in chapter 11.

The Hills have never been a static place. Higher recognition carries an obligation to absorb and adapt to the change that inevitably will come. Fences will soon keep cattle out and, perhaps, keep giraffe, eland, and other wildlife in. Six walking trails have been designed and three of these cleared. A tourist lodge may be constructed nearby. Local guides are being trained to escort visitors educationally through the sometimes precarious Hills. Whatever may occur in the future, Tsodilo will remain a place of incredible beauty and mystery, a monument to past peoples, and more often than not, each sunset will bring about the fiery copper glow on her cliffs.

A Note on Terminology

The people commonly called "Bushmen" in English or "Basarwa" by their Setswana-speaking neighbors have no overarching name for themselves. This is because the people called by this single label in reality speak many different languages, each language group having its own name for itself. Most of the languages are mutually unintelligible. This book uses the term "San" in preference to "Bushmen," except in relating stories told by the San themselves, in which they often refer to themselves as "Red people" to differentiate themselves from their Bantu-speaking neighbors, whom they refer to as "Black people," and from others, often tourists to Tsodilo, whom they refer to as "White people."

"Discovery" by the Outside World

A site inhabited for one hundred thousand years can never be "discovered." It can only be *re*-discovered, again and again, revealing new secrets to different people from farther and farther away.

David Livingstone never actually visited Tsodilo; he merely heard enough rumors to include it on one of his maps. The German geologist Siegfried Passarge arrived at Tsodilo on July 1, 1898, and over four days mapped the Hills and photographed a few paintings. In 1907 he published tracings of his photos in *Die Buschmänner der*

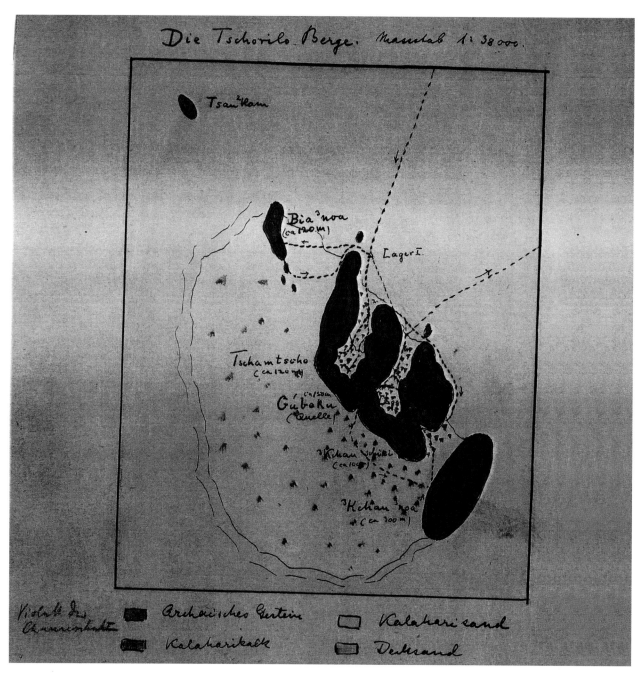

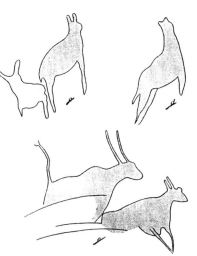

Map 0.2 (above):
Siegfried Passarge, medical doctor and geologist, was the first European to document his visit to the Hills. In four days in July, 1898, he explored the Hills and made this sketch map.

Fig. 0.9 (right):
During his visit Passarge copied some of the paintings he saw and published them in his book. The running antelope are on a cliff on the ascent into Gubekho Gorge.

Kalahahri. In 1913 Max Happe made a brief report with passing mention of the Hills. François Balsan raised the Hills' profile when over two days he photographed and prepared tracings of what has come to be known as the "Rhino Panel" on September 27–28, 1951 (**fig. 0.10**).

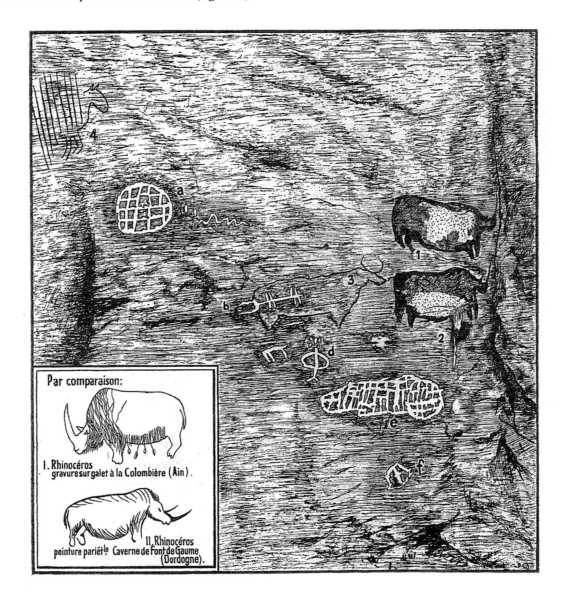

Fig. 0.10 (above):
François Balsan's "Rhino Panel".

Yet it was Laurens van der Post's book (**fig. 8.6**), *The Lost World of the Kalahari*, which brought the Hills and their art to world attention. Van der Post planned to film Tsodilo until, as he put it, the "Spirits of the Hills" intervened. His party reached Tsodilo in October 1955. On their way, a steenbok was shot, apparently a heinous crime, since they arrived, as the Spirits told van der Post through his diviner-guide, Samutshoso (Samutjau), "with blood on your hands." Van der Post believed this crime accounted for their ensuing troubles. As they raised the camera for the first time to film a magnificent eland painting, one after another its magazines jammed until finally the camera itself broke. Every dawn, bees became impossible, settling in thousands in their camp until van der Post eventually left in despair. Near the eland painting he put a bottle containing a written apology to the Spirits. Today, the curved rock face with its amazing paintings of eland, giraffe, and handprints is known as the "Van der Post Panel" (**figs. inside front cover, 0.11 & 13.1**).

Fig. 0.11 (above):
The Van der Post Panel.

Fig. 0.12 (right):
Samutjau Mukate's village in February, 1963.

Other expeditions came and went, such as the one led by Mike Hoare of mercenary fame. In 1964 archaeologists Ione and Jalmar Rudner spent a few days at the Hills, noted decorated pottery sherds, and recorded paintings. Ione published a report in the *South African Archaeological Bulletin* describing the paintings and pottery found. Yet there was still no sustained research carried out at the site. Alec Campbell first visited Tsodilo with George Silberbauer in January 1963. He relates:

> We were surprised to find almost nobody living there. We did meet Samutjau at his village, at the time just three huts were set next to the baobabs he said his father had planted **(fig. 0.12)**. He, his family and a Lozi man were the only inhabitants; nor did we see any San although remains of their abandoned shelters still stood in the gap between the Hills; they were away hunting. There were no paths, only a brooding silence by day, sounds of wind at night, and van der Post's eland, high on a rock face, gazing across the Kalahari to the western horizon. ∎

Visiting Tsodilo:
Preparing the Imagination

Alec Campbell

Trees gently undulating on sand dunes stretch into the distance in what appears to be a flat and empty world—Botswana's Kalahari Desert. Shift your eyes a little to the north and there, rising abruptly above the trees, are the Tsodilo Hills, Copper Bracelet of the Evening, a place of beauty, mystery, and enchantment.

You are standing on the main tarred road to Shakawe, just north of Sepopa village. Forty kilometers to the west, Male Hill dominates the horizon, with Female and Child Hills lying to his north. Once you have seen Male Hill, you are—like people of ten, fifty, or even ninety thousand years ago—drawn toward him, not just because he's there, but because of the incredible presence of the lone mountains rising above the sea of sand (**map 1.1**).

To reach Tsodilo from here, you once had to choose between the lesser of two evil, forty-five-kilometer, deep-sand, teeth-rattling, knuckle-whitening, three-hour endurance tests through intermittent mophane woodland, past cattle posts, grinding over and between linear dunes cut by two ancient river valleys. Some claim these hard routes "built character." Today, take the improved calcrete road from Ncamasere (**fig. 1.3**).

Fig. 1.2 (above):
The old road to Tsodilo.

Fig. 1.1 (preceding page):
Looking north with Male Hill on the right and the south end of Female Hill beyond. Upper Male Hill Mine is located in the "notch" where sunlight meets shadow.

Fig. 1.3 (above):
The new road from Ncamasere Village to Tsodilo.

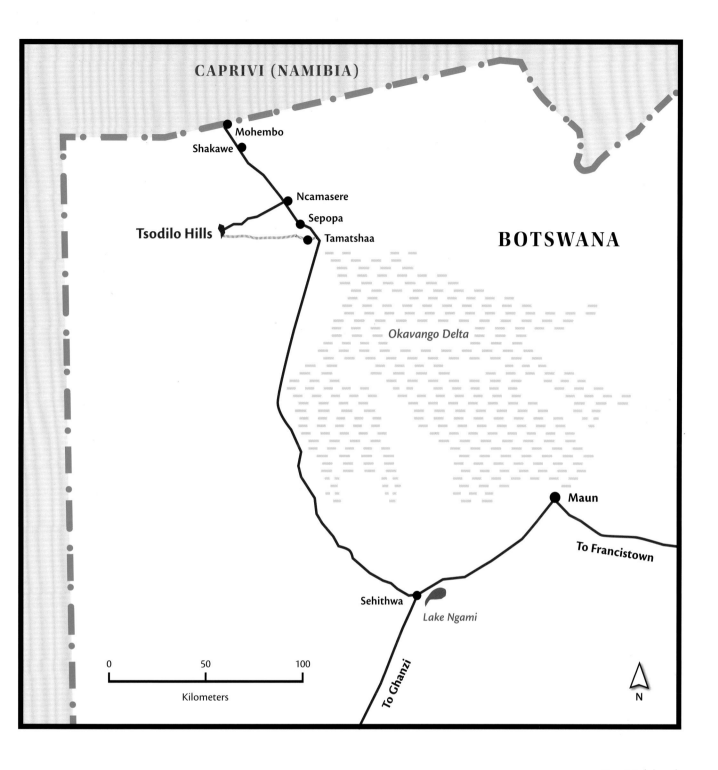

CAPRIVI (NAMIBIA)

Mohembo

Shakawe

Ncamasere

Sepopa

Tsodilo Hills

Tamatshaa

BOTSWANA

Okavango Delta

Maun

To Francistown

Sehithwa

Lake Ngami

To Ghanzi

0   50   100

Kilometers

N

Map 1.1 (above):
The old and new roads to Tsodilo.

Rock paintings and wilderness are Tsodilo's main attractions, and people travel huge distances to experience both. The Hills and the paintings are both unique. Rising hundreds of meters above the desert, the Hills stand like sentinels of the past, and the rock art fits somewhat uneasily into the category of southern Africa's "Bushman Paintings." Probably painted by Khoe herders during the first millennium, the images look more like the Northern Cape's rock engravings than the San's more conventional red fine-line art.

I have been to the Hills maybe forty or fifty times, climbed through them with Juc'hoansi and Hambukushu villagers, excavated rock shelters, mapped prehistoric mines, recorded more than four thousand rock paintings, and never tired of their splendor. I have seen the full moon rise over the copper hills, heard the wind speaking as it slithers across the rocks, and felt the presence of those who, in the distant past, hunted rhino, struggled in the mines, fished the disappearing lake, and put their thoughts and dreams in paint on the rocks.

The Final Approach

Here is a warning: as little as possible has been done to disturb nature, and the Hills remain a wilderness. The improved road ceases at Tsodilo's gate, four kilometers short of your destination (**figs. 1.1 & 1.3**). From there, you must maneuver your vehicle over sand and rough calcrete tracks. On a shallow sand ridge, resting on calcrete, you'll see the Hambukushu village. Near the clinic are a few young baobab trees (*Adansonia digitata*) and fan palm (*Hyphenae petersiana*) planted by Samutjau Mukate's father. He also planted a number of morula trees (*Sclerocarya birrea*), the largest of which now shade communal meetings in the center of the village.

Fig. 1.4 (above):
Entrance Gate to the World Heritage Site.

Driving through the entrance gate you cross the ancient lakebed, a pan formed of hard white calcrete stone that stretches to the foot of the Hills. The site museum and main campsite sit on a finger of windblown sand reaching from the foot of Gubekho Gorge westward into the lake. You need a truck, preferably with four-wheel drive; cars can't get there.

Sign in at Museum headquarters; in 2008 entry and camping were free. Here, you can wander through the thatched museum, which gives information about the Hills, buy curios made by Juc'hoansi and Hambukushu, and arrange for local guides. Water is normally available at the headquarters (although the solar-powered borehole has been known to break down), and there is an ablution block with showers and toilets. Here also is the largest campsite—a vast cleared area shaded by huge trees. Three other campsites at the south and north ends of Female Hill have no facilities. A single track runs along the west side of Male and Female Hills, giving access to these campsites. Otherwise, you walk, climb steep paths, and work your way through virgin bush.

In winter, you may see kudu, duiker, steenbok, monkeys, guineafowl, and a wide variety of birds, including Meyer's parrots, Bradfields's hornbills, and Arnot's chats. Archaeology in the rock shelters has brought up the bones of klipspringer and hyrax, but these are gone, last hunted a thousand years ago. During summer, when rains fall and the thermometer can reach 36°C, you may see elephant, wildebeest, and even roan antelope. Had you visited the Hills six thousand years ago, you would have walked along the shore of a wide lake lying against the western base of the Hills, seen rhino, buffalo, and water animals such as lechwe and sitatunga, and watched people hunting with poisoned arrows and perhaps fishing with barbed bone-pointed harpoons.

What does Tsodilo mean? Why are the Hills named Male, Female, and Child? And why does the fourth hill apparently not belong to the family? Nobody really knows the origin of the name, not even David Livingstone, creator of the earliest western map listing "Sorile," who never in fact went there. Local legends abound: "The Hills were actually born elsewhere and God moved them to their present position." Local Hambukushu call the hills *Diwe dyo Diawa* (Sheer Hills). The Juc'hoansi (San) name them *Tqxi nqum* (Copper Hills), and sometimes they extend the name to "Copper Bracelet of the Evening."

Members of a Christian church, seeking spirituality, visit the Hills, lighting candles up the steep path to the "Creation" site. When I walk through the Hills, I feel a great sense of uplift; and when I sleep there, I never forget my dreams.

A Tour on Foot

Many of the rock art sites are easy to reach. On level ground, you can walk from the site museum south along the cliff face, looking up at the rocks. First is the site with mythical antelope, a scorpion, a running hare, and "stretched" skin. In 1898, Siegfried Passarge, prospecting for minerals there, recorded in his book *Die Buschmänner der Kalahahri*, tracings of photographs he made at this site (**fig. 0.09**). Further along the cliff, look up. There, in a curved rock, facing across the desert, are paintings of eland and giraffe, and tiny handprints, the site where travel writer Laurens van der Post finally came to grief (**figs. inside front cover, 0.11 & 13.1**). Take your truck and drive across to the Male Hill and White Paintings Shelter. On the back wall are men with hands on hips, men riding horses, and an amazing white elephant (**fig. 3.1**).

Then there are the trails—Rhino Trail, Lion Trail, Cliff Trail, and others. Walking the Hills will reward your efforts, but the bush is dense, rocks look the same, directions get crossed, midday can bake, and visitors can very quickly become lost. When exploring the upper valleys, take water, snacks, and a guide. You can follow the Rhino Trail up Gubekho Gorge, looking at rock art, looking at cupules (saucer-like depressions) ground into the rock, and visiting Gubekho Spring, now usually dry. Climbing out of the gorge and following the path, step over tracks in the rock made by the first cattle or, as the Juc'hoansi claim, eland, as creatures were lowered to the earth. On the plateau, you are standing at Nqoma, where farmers rich in cattle built their villages between AD 800 and AD 1100 and traded copper jewelry from the Congo, seashells from the Atlantic, and glass beads from Asia.

Descending on the other side of the hill, you pass Snake Mine, a small, prehistoric mine dating back to at least one thousand years (**fig. 6.8**). Ten meters beyond the mine is Rhino Panel, where two extraordinary polychrome paintings of rhino merge into the cliff (**figs. 1.5 & 11.8**).

Branch from the trail and go a few hundred meters west to Ta'shra (Dancing Penises) and see a panel of paintings that apparently depicts a ceremony involving men, women, and a cow **(fig. 7.26)**.

There is a magnificent painting of a lion on the northeast projection of Male Hill **(fig. 11.4)**, paintings of elephant high on Female Hill **(fig. 0.3)**, and, in fact, paintings almost wherever you go. There are twenty-one mines where specularite, a glittering iron oxide derivative, was mined, probably first by Stone Age hunter-gatherers and then by the farmers of Nqoma. Some of the mines are large, like Greenstone Mine on the south face of Male Hill and Big Mine at the northern end of Female Hill. These specularite mines are potentially dangerous places to enter because of possible rock falls. Specularite was used in southern Africa as a cosmetic from early times. Both men and women rubbed their hair and shoulders with animal fat and then sprinkled the glittering powder on themselves **(fig. 6.9)**.

There are sacred sites at Tsodilo, hidden in the rocks, where people contacted their ancestors for help and sought for rain. The best known is the Creation site on Female Hill. Sacred even today, the Hills evoke a spirituality in both the descendants of the artists who painted them, and the many visitors who come to experience the mystery and magic of "Copper Bracelet of the Evening."

Mythology

As our investigation of Tsodilo proceeded over the course of many years we learned that not only was Tsodilo rich in scientific information about the past, but there was also a very interesting and important mythology surrounding the area. ∎

WHAT'S IN A NAME?

As mentioned previously, David Livingstone never saw the Hills, but that didn't stop him from labeling them on his 1851 map as Sorile. One modern researcher suggests that Livingstone was told the Hills were called "Sebilo," meaning "specularite" in Setswana, but misspelled the word. However, Livingstone spoke good Setswana; perhaps his informant mispronounced *sebilo*. Some forty-seven years later Passarge's guides told him they were "Tschorilo-bergen." Some say this name comes from the Setswana word *swedile*, or "damp earth," while the Wayeyi assert it is a corruption of their Shiyeyi word *shidiro*, which means "place of eating."

The Hambukushu call the collective assembly "Diwe dyo Diawa," or "Sheer Hills." Starting with the highest hill in the south and moving northward, they name them "Diwe dyo Durume" ("Male Hill"), "Diwe dyo Dikathi" ("Female Hill"), "Muanenzi" ("Child"), "Thiwe Thambuku" ("The Hill that Wants to Live by Itself"), and "Mawe o Mambirumbiru" ("Small Rocks").

The Juc'hoansi named them "Tqxi nqum," or "Copper Mountain," perhaps inspired by the reddish cliffs in the evening light. Most place names in the Hills derive from the original Ncaekhoe, such as: Male Hill, "Gtqwantqoro"; Female, "Gobekhu" (after the well at the head of the gorge above the Museum); Child, "Bienxwaa"; North Hill, "Xaunxwaa"; and the scattered rocks at the end, "Gxakwesi."

As the names imply, today's residents believe the Hills to be alive and interrelated. The Juc'hoansi who live there today have passed down over generations what they heard from the Khoe inhabitants who used to live there. They say that when their ancestors first arrived at the Hills, the Khoe explained that:

In the beginning, these Hills were people. The Male was called "Gtqwantqoro," and he was married to Xaunxwaa (North Hill). Nonetheless, Gtqwantqoro began loving Gobekhu (Female Hill), and took her as his second wife. Xaunxwaa became jealous and fought with Gtqwantqoro, and then ran away to the north. Gtqwantqoro was unhappy that she had run away, and sent his servants, Gxakwesi, to go and fetch her, but she refused and stayed where she is. Gtqwantqoro and Gobekhu then had a child, Bienxwaa. That is why today Gtqwantqoro (Male Hill) and Gobekhu (Female Hill) stay together in the south, with their child Bienxwaa (Child Hill). Xaunxwaa (North Hill) stays alone at the north, and the servants who went to call her back remain as Gxakwesi, the rocks at the very end.

~ Michael Taylor and Alec Campbell

THE POWER OF THE HILLS

In the early 1970s the renowned San scholar Megan Biesele recorded the beliefs of Tsodilo's Juc'hoansi about the power of the Hills:

Many link the origins of Tsodilo with the origin of another sacred spot quite a few miles to the east. In a place called Nqaha, north of Gumare, lies a spring at the bottom of a large depression. Tsodilo is believed to have emerged from this depression and to have traveled along a molapo *(dry river bed) to its present site. Gaoxa (God) caused this event to happen.*

Since then certain magical precautions have been observed by the Juc'hoansi in both the Tsodilo and the Nqaha areas. At neither place is a person supposed to complain if bothered by hunger, thirst, thorns, flies, or bees. He should not say he is hungry or thirsty; if a thorn lodges in his foot he should just pull it out without speaking of it or he will die; if a fly buzzes around his head he is not to wave it away or he will feel pain; if he is bitten by flies or bees he may not cry out or he will die.

What is more, it is believed that a person who drinks from the Nqaha spring without first observing the proper ceremony will die. The ceremony, conducted for traveling Juc'hoansi by the people who normally live near Nqaha, consists of tracing along the new arrival's arm, leg, and forehead with Nqaha water. The line of the tracing begins between the big toe and the next toe and travels up the leg, and between the index and third finger and travels up the arm. Attention is also paid to special spots like the throat (where the heart's pounding is visible in the pulse) and the backbone. After this observance, the new arrival may safely drink from the spring.

These precautions must be taken with the water in the spring because it is ncum, *that is, it has medicine or power. Some Juc'hoansi say that the Tsodilo Hills, too, have "drunk medicine," that they possess magical power. One woman said that on approaching Tsodilo she would first talk with the Hills so that her heart would not tremble so much that she would die.*

~ Michael Taylor and Alec Campbell

PAY RESPECT . . . OR PAY THE PRICE

For residents, Tsodilo is a sacred place inhabited by spirits of the deceased. For Hambukushu these spirits live on the tops of all the Hills and have direct access to God, or Nyambe. Juc'hoansi also believe the Hills to be possessed by spirits. Spirits demand respect, shown through careful washing procedures, devout submission, and asking permission. Those who fail, said Samutjau, pay the price:

Recently a ngaka (traditional doctor) came to visit the Hills and to collect medicine. We did not know him but offered him a guide. He refused. We explained that the Hills are dangerous and that people making their first visit must be accompanied by a guide who understand the spirits. He still refused and left alone to climb the Hills and did not come back. People went to search and found him fallen on the rocks, his head broken, dead. We reported to the police, who came to fetch the body. He was killed because he was contemptuous of the spirits. He may have been killed by Sangunguzi, a monster with one eye, one leg, and a body like a stick. He lives on Male Hill and can turn himself into a rock so that people do not recognize him. He makes people become lost and then he kills them.

*Some years ago, soldiers from the British army were contemptuous of the spirits of the Hills. They said they would climb the cliff on Male Hill. They were roped together. When they had climbed some way, the one above fell and, falling, pulled the one below from the place he was standing. The one who fell from above was killed and the one below badly hurt (**fig. 1.7**).*

~ Alec Campbell

*Fig. 1.7 (**above**): The southwestern face of Male Hill.*
White Paintings Shelter is under the outcrop to the left of the mountain.
The British soldiers are said to have fallen from a point midway up the left face.

ANCESTORS' CAVE

In 1992 Duncan Brook and Alec Campbell were climbing on the cliff near White Paintings Shelter when Duncan called to Alec, saying, "Come and look at this; I can see down into what looks like a cave." Sure enough, Duncan had climbed into a fissure and was standing on the lip of a seven-meter drop into darkness. They climbed down the cliff and found a cave entrance hidden by rocks **(fig. 1.8)**. Stepping over a loose flat rock into which cupules (small depressions) had been ground, they found more cupules on a sloping ledge and made out a single high chamber sixteen meters long and five meters wide. At the back of the chamber, they found a

Fig. 1.8 (above): Ancestors' Cave. The ledge where Hambukushu tapped a stone to attract the attention of ancestral spirits is situated to the right of the free-standing rock at the back of the cave.

second slit entrance, also concealed from outside by rocks. Later, a third tunnel entrance was found emerging just below the ledge with cupules. Later on, they brought Samutjau to ask him about the cave. He began relating:

Now that you know of this cave, I will give you its story. No, it has no particular name, nor are the paintings in the shelter below related to it. The cave was used by my ancestors when they needed help in hunting. The Juc'hoansi hunted with them, but it was only my ancestors who used the cave. Sometimes they would go hunting and would not be successful. Then they used to come to this cave. The hunters entered and one would take a stone and tap several times on this ledge (Samutjau indicated the rear ledge) to attract the attention of the ancestors. They would then ask for help in the hunt. They would then go out again to hunt and now they would be successful.

A method of hunting they used was to dig a large square pit and then build two long bush fences in the shape of a funnel with the pit at the narrow end. Animals were chased into this funnel and down the fences to fall into the pit, where they were speared to death. Yes, you can still see the outline of the pits at the northwest end of the Hills. My father showed me the holes and told me how the fences were laid out. The meat was carried to the village. Before they ate, some meat was brought to this cave. The hunter built a small fire before the ledge and cooked a little meat in a clay pot. The meat was then placed on the ledge.

Sometimes, the ancestors were asked for help and still no game was caught in the pits. Then they had to snare a small animal, a duiker perhaps, and cook the meat in a pot and give it to the ancestors before going out to hunt.

Excavating below the chamber ledge in the cave, the archaeologists found no evidence of fires. However, they did find nearly two meters of deposits near the front of the cave. The archaeologists mainly found Later Stone Age flaking debris and they obtained a radiocarbon date of about 1,800 years ago from charcoal found between eighty and ninety centimeters below the surface. An interesting find in this dated level was a piece of schist with a single depression ground into it.

Samutjau said that his grandfather had used the cave (about the 1880s), but that once his father acquired a gun the practice ceased. He showed the archaeologists an area on the plain northwest of the Female Hill that had once been cleared of trees, and that had the remains of a pit. Samutjau explained that the area had been a fenced field with a pit in the fence dug to trap animals, even rhino, coming to feed on the crops. When his ancestors moved to Nqoma in about the 1860s, the field had been abandoned.

~ Alec Campbell

I have visited the "Sex" site **(fig. 1.9)** many times accompanied by Gcau, Xauwe, Shoroka, and others. Each time I was told the story, it varied a little in detail. Juc'hoansi do not mind if people climbing the hill unknowingly step on the site but they do not want people to step on or make fun of the site if they know about it. Here is the story, not actually in the words of any single storyteller, but as I remember it being told to me:

This is a story told to us by the Ncaekhoe, the first people at Tsodilo. When we started knowing them, they told us this story. The first people lived in a village at the foot of Female Hill. They were all the same age, young adults as God had created them. They never grew older and they had no children. One day, three girls took pots and climbed up the path to the spring to collect water. They passed this spot and collected the water, put the pots of water on their heads, and started to return.

When they reached this spot, they found three boys waiting here. As they met the boys, God told them that they must have children but they replied that they did not know what He meant. So, God told them to put down their pots of water. God then molded the private parts of three women in the rock. See, here is what God molded. God then explained how the sexual act is performed using the rock He had molded. The three boys then performed the sexual act with the three girls. When they had finished, the girls picked up their pots, put them on their heads, and continued down to the village, while the boys stayed on the hill.

Fig. 1.9 (above): Xauwe recites the story attached to the Sex Site. It is the shape of the rocks in the foreground that gave the place its name.

Later, the three girls gave birth to three children and that is how the early people learned about sex and procreation. See, the evidence can still be seen in the rock.

The Sex site is above Crab Shelter and on the path that leads to the pass over the western ridge and down into the valley at the north end of Female Hill. If you are climbing to the pass and are told, "This is the site where sex started," do not walk over or sit on the site; rather move to one side, sit down, and take the opportunity to hear the story yourself.

~ Alec Campbell

TSHOKGAM, THE PYTHON SPRING

High on the lower slope of Female Hill, just below the teeth-like cliff, a deep hole in the rock holds water throughout the year and may be guarded by a dove-eating python **(fig. 1.10)**. Above and to the left of this hole lies another hole, which dries up in winter. The Ncae name is Tshokgam, although both holes are, in fact, ancient specularite mines from AD 900.

The big hole is carved at a steep angle down into the rock to a depth of between four and five meters, where it flattens outs and turns into the hill penetrating it for about six more meters. Heavy rains feed the holes from inside the hill then overflow down the hillside.

*Fig. 1.10 (**above**): Tshokgam (meaning "medicine-mouth"), also known as Python Spring and Water Hole Mine, a prehistoric specularite mine. The hole is a permanent source of water located below the cliff on Female Hill, and now used mostly by wild animals.*

Samutjau's ancestors lived on the sand ridge below the hole when they first came to the Hills; constant harassment from hungry lions forced them to move up onto Female Hill's plateau, although they still drew water from Tshokgam.

In and around the holes archaeologists found Mbukushu-style pottery sherds, a white clay bead, a light metal spear point, and blue hexagonal glass beads. Blue beads, a common European trade item, were introduced from the Angolan coast by nineteenth-century Mambari traders.

Legend has it that the python guards the hole against all predators with paws, unless they ask permission to drink. Long ago, a resident dreamt of children hunting with dogs at the well. When he awoke, he warned the children away. Nonetheless, they disobeyed him, went to hunt there, and all the dogs died, since dogs have paws.

~ *Alec Campbell*

THE HILLS AND RAIN MAKING

Some southern African researchers believe that paintings of certain mythical animals (sometimes resembling a cross between a horse and hippopotamus) represented for the artists 'rain animals' or 'rain bulls.' Modern San believe that their shamans, when 'traveling out of body,' in another reality, capture such animals, lead them across the sky and kill them above parched land to create rain. The large animals in **fig. 1.11** are not unlike those images of rain-animal paintings found in South Africa. Possibly the ancient community responsible for this painting used it in some way, either to depict a myth attached to rainmaking or actually to create rain.

When midsummer wind blows across the cliffs and through rock gaps, it makes a low noise that sounds like people talking. Tsodilo residents say the spirits are conversing around a fire on top of Male Hill.

Indeed, if the Hills are the home of Nyambe and ancestral spirits, they are also the home of the weather. One old Juc'hoansi man told Megan Biesele, "The clouds, which are all male (in other words, strong and destructive) dwell inside the Tsodilo Hills. They are like smoke and they emanate from the Hills and become the rain clouds. People fear them; even elephants are afraid of them."

The Hambukushu have had their own methods of making rain, and Samutjau

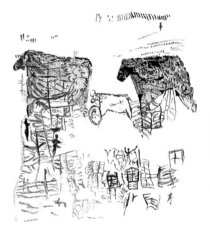

Figs. 1.11 (left) & 1.12 (below):
A domestic cow stands between two mythical animals. Lines of finger-marks stretch above and within the large animals. Four lines descend from where an udder would be on the right animal into geometric designs. A man and woman stand below the left animal. The panel may represent rain animals attracting rain and giving milk. The complete panel could represent "fertility."

once showed Alec Campbell a large fallen rock at the bottom of a cliff where the ceremony took place:

If there was a drought, adult men killed a black goat or black cow, cooked the meat, and loaded it, along with seeds of maize, sorghum, millet, beans, and melons. The eldest led the approach to the rock, barefooted and from the south. All the men passed through a gap between rock and cliff, then turned to face the rock, sat down, and greeted the ancestors. Facing the others, the elder intoned a short prayer to the spirits, begging for rain.

> "We, mama Mareka,
> Nowe gugule, nowe jwa.
> Na ku mukandera,
> Ha mutupa mvura."

> "You, mother Mareka*
> You who tells tales, you who are mighty
> I plead with you,
> For the rain has taken you to spouse."

He then climbed the rock, placed the meat on top if it, and laid the seeds beside it. From a special calabash (Samutjau used a large seashell) he sprinkled water from the Hills over the seeds, repeating the prayer. Leaving meat and seeds on the rock, the men retired from the site, back through the gap and, donning their shoes, returned to the village.

The next day the men would return to the rock and eat the meat. The remainder of the meat was cooked and divided between all the families living at Tsodilo, but only to be eaten by men and older women who had borne children.

~ Alec Campbell

* Mareka was an ancestor of Samutjau

THE SOURCE OF LIFE

Fig. 1.13 (above): Juc'hoansi and Hambukushu both believe that God made the first man and then cattle and wild animals. He lowered cattle and animals from heaven onto Female Hill. The animals left their tracks in the wet rock on the south side of Gubekho Gorge. He then painted the animals and cattle on the rocks.

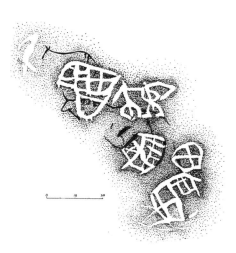

Fig. 1.14 (above): White paintings of people and geometric designs superimpose red paintings of cattle.

People in northern Botswana, eastern Namibia, and southern Angola believe Tsodilo is the place where God set the first people and animals from heaven down to earth. It was the touchstone where mankind was born, but also the place where cultures diverged. Juc'hoansi elders explained:

The first person God put on the earth was Kharac'uma. God formed him and put him down on earth at Tsodilo. Kharac'uma was the first man, and progenitor of all Red people (Khoesan). God then made cattle and wild animals and put them down too on the Female Hill at Gobekhu. God told them to go down and graze. You can see their hoof marks as they slipped in the soft rocks as they climbed down the Hills.

God then painted all the pictures that you see today on the Hills to show us the animals and people that he had made. The only picture that God did not paint was a white painting [at White Paintings Shelter] that our own ancestor Gcau painted using ash from the leadwood tree as he tried to imitate the red paintings God had made.

In the beginning there were only Red people on earth, but then God made Black people and put them on earth too. They lived together in harmony. One day Red people were out hunting and they saw cattle. In those days cattle were just like wild animals, they were not domesticated. The hunters were very excited to find animals that were so easy to hunt, as they did not run away. They went back to their Black friends to call them to come and hunt these easy animals together. When they saw the animals, the Black people laughed, and said, "No, my friends, these are cattle!" They rounded them up and took them back to their village and kept them in a kraal for themselves. That is how Red people lost cattle and ended up with only wild animals.

One day God put some leather thongs on earth, made from an eland hide. Red people and Black people saw these thongs, and thought these would be useful. They picked them up at the same time, Black people at one end, and Red people at the other. They both pulled and the thongs broke. Black people then took all the thongs. God told them, "Now you must no longer live together. Black people must go to live at the river and Red people must stay in the sandveld."

God made Red people and Black people separately. They are not related. But White people are children of Red people. This is how our grandparents told us White people came about. In the beginning, there were two Red people children who liked playing together. Their names were Tqgoma and Kanx'a. There was a certain big camelthorn tree that they always enjoyed climbing up and sitting in its branches. Their parents told them not to climb this tree as one day it would fly away with them, but they did not listen, and every day they climbed it together.

Sure enough, one day as Tqgoma and Kanx'a played up in the camelthorn tree together, it uprooted and flew off with them in its branches. It flew very far away, to another land. When the tree landed, Tqgoma and Kanx'a fell out onto the ground and died. Their bones lay on the ground for many months and whitened in the sun. Once they were completely bleached by the sun, the bones came back together and became White people. They stayed in that land and made many things, like cars and airplanes, and today they sometimes come back and visit us. That is why we say White people are the children of Red people.

~ Michael Taylor and Alec Campbell

29

The Paleoenvironment
of Tsodilo

George A. Brook

Crossing the flat sands of Botswana, even nameless hills of slight elevation provide the eye with rare and welcome relief. So Tsodilo Hills, one of the largest hill complexes in the region (figs. 2.1, 2.2 & 2.5), can't help but inspire.

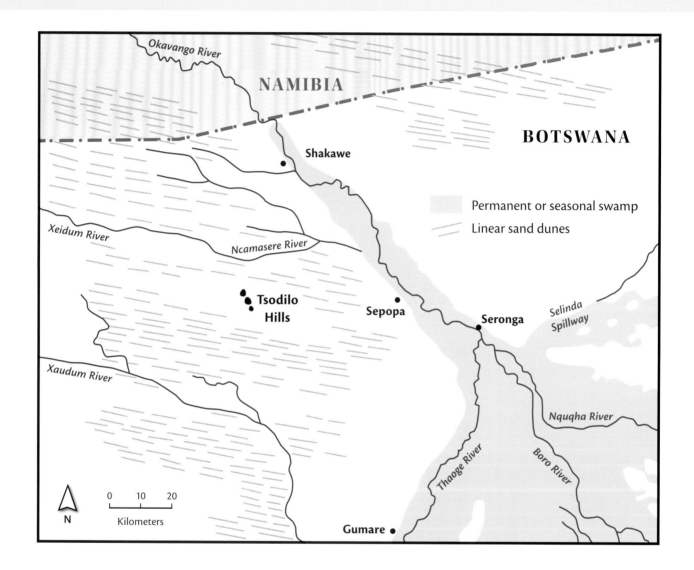

Map 2.1 (above):
Map of northwestern Botswana showing the Tsodilo Hills, the Okavango River and Delta, the major river valleys west of the Okavango, and the linear dunes. Note the absence of dunes west of Tsodilo in the wind shadow created by the Hills. Sand is piled up againts the eastern sides of the Hills.

Fig. 2.1 (preceding page):
Looking across the ancient lakebed to the forty-kilometers-long wind shadow west of the Hills.

Fig. 2.2 (above):
A view from Male Hill in about 1980. The fields of Hambukushu fill the foreground, bounded by the now disused road from Tamatshaa. On the left, sand dunes commence at the outside edge of the wind shadow created by the Hills. Beyond, tree-covered dunes stretch to the horizon.

Fig. 2.3 (right):
Satellite image of the Okavango Delta showing the dunes of the northern dune field, the Okavango River and Delta, and the Tsodilo Hills. Compare satellite image with **map 2.1**.

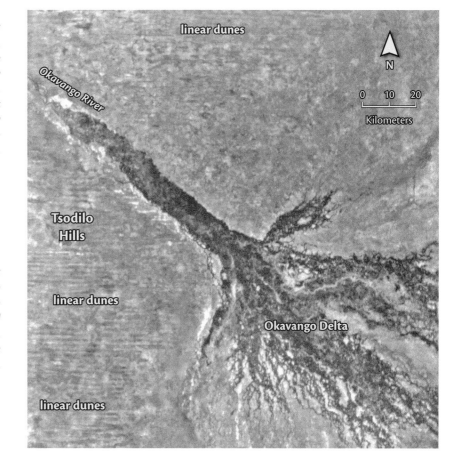

linear dunes

N

0   10   20
Kilometers

Okavango River

Tsodilo
Hills

linear dunes

Okavango Delta

linear dunes

The top of the Male Hill reaches 1,395 meters above sea level and from base to top it is about 385 meters. It offers a spectacular view in all directions, but mankind cannot live on vistas. We need food, shelter, and water. Except for a series of small seeps and springs, there is no surface water for game or people. Yet several important archaeological sites and four thousand rock paintings testify to how important the Hills were to Middle Stone Age, Later Stone Age and Iron Age human inhabitants. What brought people here, and how did they remain?

Geological and paleo-environmental data offer us some early clues. There is evidence of both much wetter and much drier conditions than today. Up to twelve thousand years ago an ancient lake and wetlands could have provided sustenance year-round. Even in times of greater aridity there was seepage water and pockets of wells. If one knew where to look, there was food and water, but the Hills during the dry periods would have been visited infrequently.

To a large degree, environmental factors combined with natural selection and other mechanisms of evolution dictate the pace and parameters of human evolution. Today scientists study climate flux, especially global warming, to anticipate

Fig. 2.4 (above):
The Female Hill complex viewed from the top of the Male Hill. The quartzites and schists are dissected into blocks by weathering along NNE-SSW and NW-SE fractures. The calcretes, which delimit the floor of the former lake, are visible at lower left and eolian sand piled up against the eastern slopes of the hill complex to the right.

Fig. 2.5 (above):
The calcrete shoreline of the ancient lakebed is clearly visible in front of the cattle.

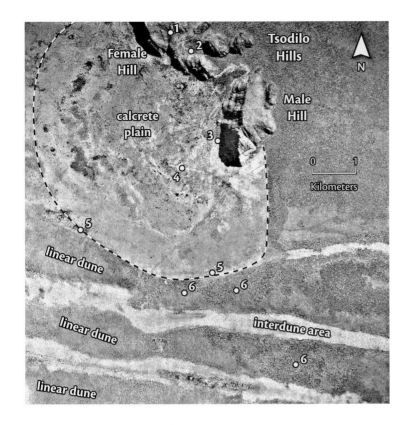

Fig. 2.6 (above):
Aerial photograph of the Male and Female Hills showing the maximum extent of the former lake to the southwest. The dashed line shows the shoreline of the lake as it was nineteen thousand to twelve thousand years ago.
1 = Divuyu Village; 2 = Nqoma Village; 3 = White Paintings Shelter;
4 = the Tsodilo Hills airstrip; 5 = sites with ages for the ancient lake shoreline;
6 = sites with ages for the dune sands.

Fig. 2.7 (above):
Calcrete from three hundred meters southwest of Male Hill broken open to show embedded mollusk shells.

our immediate future. Here we examine the hard evidence to understand the prehistoric climate and appreciate how it affected our human ancestors.

Lakes and Rivers: Evidence of a Wetter Climate

Tsodilo is semi-arid, but it wasn't always so. To the southeast of the Male and Female Hills lies a flat hard plain of about 5 x 8 kilometers (**figs. 2.4, 2.5 & 2.6**). The plain extends all the way to the vegetated linear dune in the south, and is formed by a layer of calcium carbonate, or calcrete. Today it holds an airstrip. Millennia ago it held a shallow lake.

Fossil mollusk shells and fossil diatoms from freshwater algae are found in the calcrete; they indicate ancient deposition from standing water probably nowhere more than five to seven meters deep (**tables 2.1 & 2.2**). This prehistoric lake once lapped against the basal slopes of the Male and Female Hills to the north and east. In the south wave action eroded a curved shoreline into the northernmost linear dune (**fig. 2.6**).

All thirteen fossil freshwater mollusk species discovered in the calcrete still occur in the Okavango River system today (**table 2.1 & fig. 2.8**). Seven require air and would have been linked with aquatic plants in shallow-water environments, typical of lake margins. Five extract oxygen from the water, live in bottom sediments, and live longer, and so require more permanent water bodies. One, *Melanoides tuberculata*, can't survive in ephemeral water bodies.

What can we learn from lowly mollusks? We can infer what may have made people sick. *Biomphalaria pfeifferi* hosts the parasite causing intestinal

Table 2.1: Mollusk species in lacustrine carbonates at Tsodilo Hills		
FAMILY		
Prosobranchia	**Pulmonata**	**Lamellibranchia**
Bellamya capillata	Lymnaea natalensis	Corbicula c.f. fluminalis
Pila occidentalis	Afrogyrus/Ceratophallus sp	
Lanistes sp	Ceratophalus sp	
Melanoides tuberculata	Biomphalaria pfeifferi	
Melanoides victoriae	Bulinus c.f. globosis	
	Bulinus depressus	
	Bulinus tropicus	

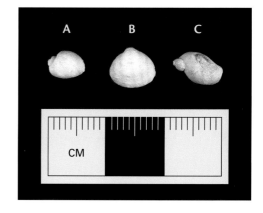

Fig. 2.8 (above):
Selected mollusk shells recovered from lake carbonate deposits southwest of the Male Hill. A = Bulinus depressus; B = Corbicula c.f. fluminalis; C = Lymnaea natalensis.

schistosomiasis, while *Biomphalaria globosis* and *Biomphalaria africanus* host the parasite causing urinal schistosomiasis (bilharzias). Since all three species are present in the lacustrine carbonates at Tsodilo we might presume that peoples living in this area when lakes were present might have suffered from these diseases caused by flatworms known as schistosomes.

The impressive local fossil diversity of thirteen mollusk and sixteen diatom species bears witness to a permanent, shallow, warm lake that varied seasonally in area and depth, with desiccation only on peripheries. Based on the spatial distribution of mollusk and diatom species, we can infer that the lake was deepest and most permanent just west of the Male Hill close to the site of White Paintings Shelter. In the south and east, the lake was shallow with dense aquatic vegetation. Diatoms discovered in calcretes southwest of the Child Hill suggest that a seasonal water body also previously existed there.

How long ago? Five radiocarbon ages on mollusk shells range from 13,750 to 36,100 years ago; a sixth dates to older than 41,000 years. The calcrete matrix in the lake deposit at the Child Hill is at least 25,500 years old. Where the lake eroded the linear dune in the south, the sands along the shoreline have provided ages in the range of 11,800 to 18,400 years (**fig. 2.6**). The deep part of the lake goes back from 40,000 up to perhaps 32,000 years ago,

Table 2.2: Diatom species in lacustrine carbonates at Tsodilo Hills				
FAMILY				
Benthic (bottom-dwelling) species			**Planktonic (surface-dwelling) species**	
Naviculaceae	**Epithemiaceae**	**Bacillariaceae**	**Thalassiosiraceae**	**Fragilariaceae**
Mastoglia elliptica dansei	Denticula tenuis	Nitzschia lancelettula	Stephanocyclus meneghiniana	Fragilaria pinnata
Encyonema muelleri	Denticula kuetzingii	Nitzschia denticula		Psuedostaurosira brevistriata
Diploneis elliptica	Rhopalodia gibbuleria			
Gomphonema 2 sp	Epithemia sorex			
Cymbella cymbiformis	Epithemia zebra			
Cymbella cistula				

with diatom evidence suggesting that conditions became more seasonal after 36,000 years ago. Overall, data indicate that lacustrine conditions predominated over two stages, from 27,000 to 22,000 and 19,000 to 12,000 years ago. These periods correlate well with evidence from caves, pans, and lakes elsewhere in Botswana and neighboring Namibia, where wet intervals have been documented at 41,000 to 33,000, 28,000 to 26,000, and 20,000 to 14,000 years ago. Since no large surface streams enter the Tsodilo basin, the lake must have been fed largely by groundwater seepage. Water levels rose and fell slowly, rather than suddenly.

The Absence and Presence of Fish

From the fossil evidence we may also infer absence or presence of other aquatic species. Conspicuous by their absence are the larger common gastropods and bivalves of the Okavango, which at the larval stage are an obligatory parasite of fish. The missing larger mollusks could mean that there were no fish in Lake Tsodilo to host them. However an alternative possibility is that there were fish but the large mollusks had not reached or could not survive in the lake waters. At Lake Turkana in Kenya, for example, there are no bivalves because of the high salinity, yet there are a large number of fish species. In the next chapter we will see that the people who lived at Tsodilo clearly ate fish. Ancient bones indicate that fish was a dietary staple, which begs the question of where these fish came from.

Just forty kilometers to the northeast, the permanent Okavango River flowed even during arid climatic intervals, and so could have been exploited by early peoples living at Tsodilo at any time in the past. Eighty kilometers is a rather long walk to fetch and return with a regular supply of food, though. However, only fifteen kilometers north of Tsodilo the Xeidum/Ncamasere River "flows" from west to east, parallel to the linear dunes. In the west the river is called Xeidum, while from east of Tsodilo over to the Okavango River it is known as the Ncamasere (**map 2.1**). The South African administration of Namibia constructed a dam across the river in Namibia long before independence, thus creating a reservoir and terminating the Xeidum's flow into Botswana. The remains of reed beds can still be seen in this river in Botswana.

Today you won't see a trickle or even a damp patch. Water comes only from wells dug into the sands of the riverbed; there is rarely west-to-east surface flow even during the height of the summer wet season. Only during seasonal floods of the Okavango might water push briefly back up into the Ncamasere.

Oral history of peoples living at Tsodilo relates that not too long ago, after heavy rains, the Xeidum indeed flowed from the west and that when the big floods built up in the Okavango, water backed up in the Ncamasere and the waters met, creating a continuous stretch of water from the Okavango to the Xeidum from late April through June. Studies of sediments in the Xeidum suggest more rainfall in the area in the past, and that west-east surface flow was more common before about four thousand years ago. Since then there has been a gradual filling of the valley floor by organic and other sediments in depressions carved out by the flowing stream, with eventual burial by eolian (windblown) sands.

To conserve energy and increase survival, it seems likely that during wetter periods of the past, people fished and hunted along the Xeidum/Ncamasere, and possibly also at Lake Tsodilo, rather than trekking to the more distant Okavango, bringing at least some of the food back to Tsodilo to cook, share, trade, and consume. Buried in the sands of rock shelters in the area we find further evidence to support exactly that.

The Rock Shelter Record of Change

The Depression Rock Shelter and Rhino Cave are fissure-like openings produced by weathering along NW-SE joints. Large rock shelters like White Paintings are produced by preferential weathering along vertical and steeply dipping fractures, the latter inclined to the northeast. In addition, preferential chemical weathering at the base of the hill, where water accumulates after rain, undercuts slopes, making them unstable, particularly in areas where joints are frequent. In this way large blocks can be dislodged from the hill slope, resulting in the formation of rock overhangs or shelters.

Sediments in the caves and rock shelters are dominated by eolian, or windblown, sand units deposited rapidly during arid intervals. Separating these units are thin layers of coarser, more angular sediments produced by weathering of the bedrock in and near the rock shelter, and near the surface buried soil horizons. The coarser deposits are evidence of reduced eolian activity, and increased vegetation cover on the nearby linear dunes. In addition, increased chemical and mechanical weathering of the bedrock indicates substantially wetter and less windy conditions. Excavations have revealed ten eolian units in seven meters of deposits that span the period from the present through the Later Stone Age and into the Middle Stone Age, covering the last hundred thousand years at White Paintings Shelter **(fig. 2.5)**, the only rock shelter so far known in the entire Kalahari that at times directly overlooked a lake.

Significantly, deposits at White Paintings contained fish bones, mostly *Claridae* (catfish) and *Cichlidae* (perch-like fish, or bream) **(fig. 2.9)**. In the upper three meters there were also bones of wetland animals such as reedbuck, lechwe, bushbuck, bushpig, and Angoni vlei rat. There were also bones of ducks, geese, and white-breasted cormorant. Greater numbers of bones of less water-reliant species like impala, kudu, roan antelope, and hartebeest/tsessebe indicate more moisture and improved pasture conditions for these animals.

Fig. 2.9 (above):
Fish bones and pieces of harpoon points recovered from the upper fish level,
dated between nine thousand and seven thousand years ago in White Paintings Shelter.

Fish vertebrae from White Paintings have been dated to 9,000 to 7,000 years ago; other evidence shows active occupation 10,000 to 4,000 years ago. There is no evidence of a lake during this later period. Greater flow along the Xeidum implies more rainfall but not enough to feed a lake at Tsodilo.

Phytodendron rautanenii Schinz, also known as *Schinzophton rautanenii* or mongongo, is a large fruit-bearing tree of the family Euphorbiaceae. The nuts and fruit are an important wild food staple in the Kalahari, but survive only in a narrow climate range from 350 to 750 millimeters annual rainfall. The presence or absence of this food in the fossil record helps complete our picture of the prehistoric climate at Tsodilo. Mongongo nut fragments have been discovered at all of the shelters, yet none were found at Depression Shelter between 110 to 140 centimeters, or 4,700 to 7,500 years ago, raising the possibility that conditions were not suitable for the trees at that time. The lack of nuts during the above time span, when combined with evidence of fish exploitation and a flowing Xeidum River, suggests that annual rainfall during this period was more than 750 millimeters, or, outside the climatic range of the trees.

The Geological Formation of Tsodilo

To set the stage, go back long before the rock art, mines, carvings, people, or even existence of the actual Hills, to a time of shifting, unconsolidated sands in the Precambrian period 700 to 630 million years ago. These sands and associated heavy minerals metamorphosed and deformed during the early Paleozoic, around 560 million years ago, producing the foliated, mica-rich quartzites that we see today. The powerful chisel of ice began to sculpt these Damara rocks during the late Carboniferous-Permian glaciation (not to be confused with the Pleistocene Ice Age 300 million years later).

Kalahari Group sediments of Cretaceous (136 million years old) to recent age were deposited over those earlier rocks and today mantle the area around the Hills **(figs. 2.2 & 2.4)**. These sediments may be 100 to 200 meters thick and include conglomerates and gravel, marl, sandstone, alluvium, lacustrine, or lake deposits, unconsolidated windblown Kalahari sand, and duricrusts. Duricrusts accumulate iron deposits, commonly known as ferricrete, silica (silcrete), and calcium carbonate (calcrete), that either rest on top of preexisting sediments or cement within them. The processes result in indurated masses from a few centimeters to tens of meters thick.

The Hills are arranged in offset ridges that run parallel to the dominant NNE-SSW vertical joint direction. NW-SE vertical joints divide these ridges into a series of large joint blocks **(figs. 2.4 & 2.10)**. A third system of joints dips to the NE at angles of 25 to 50 degrees, and weathering along these leads to the detachment of large joint blocks from the hillsides. The foliation in the quartzites is due to concentrations of minerals such as epidote and muscovite. An older layering may represent original banding, rarely more than a few millimeters thick, rich in specularite **(fig. 6.2)** and rutile. Visible quartz veins are ten centimeters thick but locally may form zones up to six meters thick and may include a number of secondary minerals: mostly muscovite with some kyanite, hematite, and tourmaline.

Isolated hills of crystalline rock that rise from a flat plain are called inselbergs. In Botswana they occur where Kalahari Group sediments are shallow, allowing resistant, upstanding areas of older rocks beneath to project through to the surface. Inselbergs form because the dense rocks have no pores to absorb rainfall; runoff is restricted to infrequent open joints and faults. Such hard masses resist chemical breakdown and endure long after the softer and more heavily fractured rocks surrounding them erode.

Over time they remain as hills in a flat landscape and grow more resistant to erosion because they shed soils that could hold water to the rock, bring about chemical weathering, or allow vegetation to take root in cracks. The result, as at Tsodilo, are steep scarps, rock overhangs, and exposed quartzite faces, right down to the bases, just waiting for the creative spark of human painters, carvers, stone workers, and miners who would one day arrive at this dramatic stage.

Hydrology: Water Sculpts Tsodilo's Habitat

Humans may live for weeks without roots, nuts, fruit, fish, or meat. In Botswana's heat we die in three days without water.

That immutable fact makes water the most critical resource at Tsodilo, and explains why and how it shaped human evolution here, governing migration, health, trade, diets, perhaps even religion and culture. Indeed, the significance of the location of water during the past may even be seen in the placement of some rock paintings, marked by natural water seepage stains directly on the rock face. Yet to appreciate how water shaped the people of Tsodilo, we must first grasp how the physical landscape shaped, and was shaped by, water itself.

Kalahari Group sediments form the regional groundwater aquifer in the Tsodilo region. In fact, the water table is at relatively shallow depth; in historic times, before modern industrial drilled boreholes, a hand-dug well in the calcrete plain south of the Hills provided water for local inhabitants at just two meters deep.

In inter-dune and low-lying areas near Tsodilo, underlain by impermeable calcrete and silcrete duricrusts, rainfall may pond briefly before evaporating. Surprisingly, most recharge to the regional aquifer occurs through the

Fig. 2.10 (above):
North end of Female Hill in foreground; Child Hill lies in middle ground and North Hill is just visible in background.
Clearly visible are the offset ridges that run parallel with the NNE-SSW vertical joint direction.

dune sands that absorb rainfall rapidly and retard evaporation. As the dunes contain water at shallow depth, they support open bush and tree savanna, dominated by *Burkea africana* and *Pterocarpus angolensis*. By contrast, inter-dune areas with limited groundwater reserves are covered by grasses and sparse shrubs. Some of the water entering the dune sands ultimately makes its way deeper into the Kalahari Group aquifer.

A second source of water is in the Damara quartzites of the Hills. After rain, some water seeps into open fractures in the bedrock and migrates vertically and horizontally along cracks and openings until it emerges on the sides or base of the hill. These seeps can produce visible spring flow at the surface, as is the case south of the sites of the Iron Age settlements of Divuyu and Nqoma. More commonly they produce small pools in the floors of enlarged fissures shaded from the sun, which slows evaporation.

These pools, high in the Hills, are difficult to access but because they are more or less permanent, in the past they remained a critical source of water during the dry season. Knowledge of the reliability of such springs and seeps and their exact location was valuable information that could be shared or traded by inhabitants and visitors. Some pools remain today, but are so hidden that few know of them. On Female Hill a pool at the base of a specularite mine known as Tshokgam (Water Hole Mine) has been an important traditional source of water for people, who share the water with wild birds, monkeys, pythons, and leopards. Samutjau's ancestors lived below the waterhole in the 1860s–70s. Today, the water is valued and used by some members of the Zion Christian Church.

Stories in the Sands:
Dunes Provide Evidence of a Drier, Windier Climate

Broad parallel sand ridges surround Tsodilo as part of an extensive linear dune field in the northern Kalahari (**map 2.1 & fig. 2.4**). A hard, close look at their shape and character reveals stories in the sands.

Linear dunes develop or enlarge either when winds blow sand from two dominant directions or when wide unimodal winds sculpt them from one part of the compass. Depending on the wind regime, the dunes may have one or two slip faces perpendicular to the main long axis of their spine.

None of the dunes "migrate" as a whole; grains of sand merely pass downwind along their lengths. That's what happened in Tsodilo's drier, windier past. The dunes are oriented from east to west, and sand piled along the eastern margin of the Hills indicates that the dunes were formed by winds blowing from the east. As the Hills deflected those eastern winds to the north and south, they formed a dune-free "wind-shadow" extending fifty kilometers west of the Hills (**map 2.1**).

Today, west and northwest of the Okavango Delta, dune ridges stand remarkably straight, rise up to twenty-five meters high, are spaced 1.0 to 2.5 kilometers apart, and continue for more than two hundred kilometers (**map 2.1 & fig. 2.4**). Immediately south of Tsodilo the dunes have subdued and rounded crests and rise only about ten meters above inter-dune areas.

Active linear dunes, like those in the Namib Desert, are still being moved by the wind. What about the northern dunes at Tsodilo? Recently they have been extensively degraded by non-eolian processes and support a dense vegetation cover. Grains are rounded to subrounded and under the microscope appear frosted and pitted due to chemical etching by water.

In addition, surface sand is pale, light-yellowish brown but at shallow depth the grains are orange to red (**fig. 2.1**). The color is due to a thin layer of chemically precipitated iron oxide, or rust, and comes from dust and weathering of iron-rich minerals within the sand matrix. Sand reddening indicates sand stability; transport sheds the iron coat. In short, only the light brown surface sands keep moving, while the red dune cores sit still. The degraded dunes, the red sands, and the dense vegetation cover all confirm that Tsodilo's dune field is no longer active.

Yet recent dating suggests they used to be, in the intervals 115,000–95,000, 46,000–41,000, 32,000–30,000, and 16,000–13,000 years ago. Sand samples recovered from 0.7–1.75 meters depth beneath the crests of the two linear dunes immediately south of the Male and Female Hills fall squarely within the 32,000–30,000 year period of dune activity. A sample from 4.9 meters depth fits well into the 115,000–95,000 year period of dune development. This age taken from midway down the total dune profile indicates that the dune started developing long before 98,000 years ago, as by then at least 4 meters of sand had accumulated.

Green Life on Rock and Sand

Tsodilo rises out of a field of linear dunes aligned east-to-southeast and west-to-northwest that stretch from the Okavango Delta westward into Namibia. From high on Male or Female Hill at sunrise or sunset, you have a wonderful view of these dunes swelling one beyond the other like waves at sea (**fig. 2.2**). The dunes can rise to a height of twenty-five meters, once even higher.

The tops of the dunes are well wooded by red syringa (*Burkea africana*), weeping wattle (*Peltophorum africanum*), silver leaf (*Terminala sericea*), Kalahari apple-leaf (*Lonchocarpus nelsii*), large-fruited bush willow (*Combretum zeyheri*), crotons, and acacias. The sand ridge against the east side of the Hills also includes trees such as blood-wood (*Pterocarpus angolensis*), large false mopane (*Guibourtia coleosperma*), and Rhodesian teak (*Baikiaea plurijuga*).

The vegetation on the Hills differs markedly from that on both the dunes and the lakebed. Crotons, combretums, and commiphoras are common, but most important is the wide variety of fruit trees which include baobab, marula, mongongo, false brandy-bush and other grewia species, sour plum, jackal berry (*Diosporos mespiliformis*), African mangosteen (*Garcinia livingstonei*), bird plum (*Berchemia discolor*), monkey orange (*Strychnos cocculoides*), and white bauhinia (*Bauhinia petersiana*).

Among other edible plants are a wide variety of berries, melons, cucumbers, and roots, and numerous medicinal and magical trees, shrubs, vines, and herbs. Of particular interest is the lucky-bean creeper (*Abrus*

Fig. 2.11 (above):
Lucky beans (Abrus precatorius) are used as charms for success, as well as in jewelry-making.

precatorius) **(fig. 2.11)** found also in West Africa and there said that four beans weigh a "carat," the ancient measure for weighing gold dust. Nowhere else within one hundred kilometers of Tsodilo is there such a wonderful variety of plants, particularly edible and medicinal species. From December to April beware of painful nettles found in the valleys and gorges and known locally as *sebabatsane*.

The Ancient Lakebed

The lakebed indents the sand ridge to the south of Male Hill and stretches along the foot of the western cliffs almost to North Hill. At a number of places, fairly narrow, low sand ridges commence against the cliffs and point westward into the lakebed.

From the Hills, a low sand ridge about five kilometers distant and running more or less parallel to the Female Hill marks the western boundary of the old lake. Some areas of the lakebed are now covered by sand, but it once extended over at least forty square kilometers and may have been several meters deep.

To the west of Tsodilo, stretching for some forty kilometers is a sand shadow **(fig. 2.1)**, an almost flat area where the Hills have prevented windblown sand from forming dunes. Vegetation is similar to that on the dunes although trees do not achieve any real height.

Temperatures vary considerably: winter nights sometimes bring frosts, then during the day it can heat up to 30°C. Summer noon reaches over 36°C, with warm nights. Rainfall averages 560 millimeters annually, most falling during the hot summer months between November and March. Today after heavy rainfall, areas of the lakebed still flood, sometimes to a depth of ten to fifteen centimeters, although the water soon disappears. ■

Large trees such as leadwood (*Combretum imberbe*), rain-tree (*Lonchocarpus capassa*) and knobthorn (*Acacia nigrescens*) can reach great height and sometimes girths on the lakebed opposite the southern end of Female Hill. There are numerous fruit-bearing bushes on the lakebed's sand ridges, such as false brandy-bush (*Grewia bicolor*), used for making an alcoholic beverage known locally as *mogwana*, and sour plum (*Ximenia spp.*), ideal for quenching the thirst.

Today, few large species of wild animals remain in and around Tsodilo, although this was not the case in the past. Once, giraffe, eland, impala, and rhinoceros were common visitors, but they are gone. Elephants coming from the Okavango River still visit the Hills for short periods during the rains, but the last rhino was probably shot in 1935. A few roan antelope survive on the dunes, while African wild dog, wildebeest, and zebra occasionally pass through the area. If you're lucky you may hear the distant roar of lions.

Kudu and monkeys inhabit both the dunes and the Hills, while leopards have eaten goats and dogs from the village. Duiker and steenbok occupy the dunes and lakebed, but are rarely seen in the Hills. In the 1970s, two male baboons lived on Female Hill, but they are gone without replacements.

There are numerous nocturnal animals, although they are rarely seen: aardvark, brown hyena, pangolin, genets, serval, civet, galago, jackals, and springhare.

After heavy rains, flocks of storks and even pink-backed pelican have been seen on Tsodilo's flooded lakebed and pans; palmnut and white-headed vultures may be present along with a wide variety of eagles. Ostriches, once plentiful, are now rare, but other large ground-walking birds include Kori bustards, ground hornbills, and secretary-birds. The dryland grey- and brown-hooded and woodland

Fig. 2.12 (above): Knobthorn (Acacia nigrescens) *was apparently used by Tsodilo's prehistoric miners to build fires against and crack hard rock faces so that the specularite could be extracted.*

Fig. 2.13 (above): Bull kudu feeding in thick bush.

Fig. 2.14 (above): Secretary bird (Sagittarius serpentarius) with chick in nest hidden in the crown of an acacia tree. These birds inhabit the few open grasslands to the west of the Hills.

kingfishers eat insects. Keep an eye out for Bradfield's hornbill (fairly common among the usual yellow-billed, red-billed, and grey hornbills), the rare black-faced babbler, and the yellow-billed oxpecker.

Snakes, common but rarely seen, include quill-snouts, grass- or sand-snakes, Mopani snakes (which climb trees), and the python, which can inflict a nasty wound with its teeth. It's not poisonous, but others are: black mambas, cobras, puff adders, horned adders, boomslangs, and stilettos.

Among other reptiles, you may see the monitor lizard, legless skinks, Bibron's gecko (local belief holding it to be poisonous—not in the conventional sense, but rather that if it did bite it will induce such hysteria that one might well die laughing), and the endemic Tsodilo rock gecko (*Pachydactylus tsodiloensis*). Hinged Kalahari, geometric, and leopard tortoises —so long and so regularly collected and eaten that they are now protected by law—may appear on the lakebed and dunes, while the Cape terrapin survives in the pans to the southwest.

Scorpions and centipedes urge care when gathering wood, moving stones, or dismantling camp. During the rainy season, mosquitoes, ticks, and biting flies can be a nuisance, and bees can become a positive menace. After periods of little or no rain, bees swarm into visitors' camps seeking moisture, and can settle in thousands on damp areas, open food, and water containers. They only sting if provoked; so move slowly and keep sweet or wet stuff under cover and lids and tents closed.

~ Alec Campbell

Westerners used to think it quaint that Tsodilo residents use a variety of natural medicines gathered from the bush. That was before they spent billions buying derivatives of hoodia, an appetite suppressant brought to outside attention by the San, who have used it for millennia on hunts. Now bio-prospectors and amateurs alike pay closer attention.

Bush medicine can be divided into those with direct therapeutic action, such as *mokgalo* leaves (*Ziziphus mucronata*), chewed and used as a poultice to draw pus from boils, and those with magical powers, such as eagle feces, employed in rain-making. Some have both. Hambukushu use small oval clay wasps' nests (*zezebe*) to appease the anger of deceased ancestors; Juc'hoansi use it to cure pains in the pit of the stomach (*setshwabo*).

Common minor ailments with quick recovery are usually believed to have natural causes. More serious sicknesses such as cancer, stroke, blindness, and heart failure are caused by the ill will of neighbors or ancestors and require the attention of a diviner, who determines causes and recommends cures. Diviners may use gemsbok horn filled with medicines or an inverted calabash twisted on a cloth. Questions are asked and the horn pushed through the sand or the calabash twisted. Resistance answers the diviner's questions, which mainly seek to expose hidden animosity between patient and others.

Guides may indicate medicinal plants and explain their uses, among them:

- *Gxara* (in *Juc'hoan*). Hambukushu use the sap in the pods to heal dry, cracked skin. The raw sap is spread across the cracks on fingers and feet. Juc'hoansi eat the caterpillars that feed on the tree.

- *Sengaparile* (*Harpargophytum procumbens*). Tubers are dried, ground, and used as a tea for high blood pressure and arthritis. Europeans market the plant as "Devil's Claw."

- *Moithimodiso* (*Cotyledon orbiculata*). Used to induce sneezing and cure headaches. Roots are burnt and inhaled by a man who has slept with a woman who has suffered a miscarriage. The dried hollow stem is used to suck water from cavities in trees.

- *Moologa* (*Croton gratissimus*). Seeds used as a laxative.

- *Mogonono* (*Terminalia sericea*). Bark of the root is stamped, soaked in water, and fed to expectant cows to prevent miscarriage.

- *Moroka* (*Commiphora mossambicensis*). Ash from the burnt bark is used to cure wounds in cattle.

- *Mouna*. A many-stemmed short evergreen bush with red edible fruits. Roots are boiled and the water drunk to cure diarrhea.

- *Mosokelatsebeng* (*Sanseveria spp.*). Roots are cut to a point, inserted into the ear, and twisted, the sap abating tinnitus **(fig. 2.15)**.

- *Seolo sa bonyonyo*. Black ant-heap earth taken from cracks in the rocks. The earth is warmed in the fire and rubbed on painful parts of the body.

- *Motawana* (*Capparis tormentosa*). Green shrub often found on anthills. When digging the roots, blood must be spilled into the excavation. Ground-up roots are mixed with other medicines to strengthen them. Water in which the root has been boiled is used to alleviate malaria.

~ Michael Taylor, Alec Campbell and Niall Campbell

Fig. 2.15 (left):
Sansevieria or bow-string hemp (Sansevieria aethiopica). The root is shaped to a point and gently twisted in the ear to cure tinnitus; hence the Tswana name mosekelatsebeng (twist in the ear). Thin strands of fibre removed from the leaves are rolled to form a thin strong string; hence the common English name.

Fig. 2.16 (below):
Baobab fruit (Adansonia digitata). The white pith around the seeds, sometimes known as "cream-of-tartar," when soaked makes an acidulous drink used to subdue the effects of fever.

Tsodilo is famous for its wealth of edible plants, and both Juc'hoansi and Hambukushu continue to collect wild foods despite changing attitudes and tastes toward conventional flour, sorghum, millet, mealie-meal, sugar, tea, and canned drinks. They collect and store some fruits, but eat others, like *moretologa* plums (*Ximenia* spp.), when passing by. Important fruits include:

- *Mongongo* (*Phytodendron rautanenii*). Fruit containing a hard nut with a kernel of calorific value equivalent to soya beans. The kernels are broken from their shells and roasted in sand under hot charcoal.

- *Morula* (*Sclerocarya birrea*). Fruit containing a hard nut with a kernel of high calorific value. The flesh is eaten and the kernel is roasted.

- *Mokgalo* (*Ziziphus mucronata*). As well as being medicinal, the berries are eaten ripe. In the past they were dried and stored, then ground to make meal.

- *Motsentsela* (*Berchemia discolor*). Large tree with small edible fruit.

- *Motsaodi* (*Garcinia livingstonei*). Ever-green tree with fleshy edible fruits.

- *Leketa*. Small annual plant with pointed leaves boiled as a relish for porridge.

- *Mogwana* (*Grewia bicolor*). Shrub with berries used to make an alcoholic drink also called *khadi*.

- *Mogorogorwana* (*Strychnos cocculoides*). An orange-sized fruit with a fleshy interior that contains high levels of strychnine until it ripens, when it is a tasty food.

- *Leboa*. A mushroom that is boiled and sometimes dried.

- *Seboko sa mongana* (Acacia caterpillar). Boiled or roasted.

- *Serotelakgamelo*. Heavy black-and-yellow beetle eaten raw.

- *Kokobele* or *Ntlhwa*. Flying ants or termites, usually roasted before consumption.

- *Nato*. Edible caterpillar found on *monato* (*Burkea africana*).

Fig. 2.17 (above): Mumbukushu woman de-winging termites at Tamatshaa. The termites are sold and eaten, usually fried in their own fat, or on a piece of zinc left lying in the sun.

- *Sethithi*. Large white edible grub found in rotten wood and cattle manure. Delicious!
- *Tsie*. Locust, usually roasted.

Poisons:

- *Polyclada flexuosa*. The *morula* beetle, whose pupae are used for arrow poison.
- *Motsebe* (*Croton megalobotrys*). Used to poison fish.
- *Seroka* (*Commiphora schimperi*). Berries used as a poison.

~ Alec Campbell

Fig. 2.19 (above): Corky-bark monkey orange (Strychnos cocculoides). When eaten unripe, the fruit can cause vomiting; after ripening, it is delicious. The seeds contain strychnine and should not be swallowed.

Fig. 2.18 (above): Blue sourplum (Ximenia americana). The fruit is sour but refreshing to taste. Most people spit out the skin which is unpleasant. The kernel is oily and avoided, believed to be slightly poisonous.

Fig. 2.20 (right): Large false mopane seeds (Guibourtia coleosperma). The red seeds are roasted under coals and chewed, or pounded into meal. The fruit is sometimes used to make a non-alcoholic drink.

Windows into the Past:
Excavating Stone Age Shelters

Larry Robbins,
Mike Murphy, and
Alec Campbell

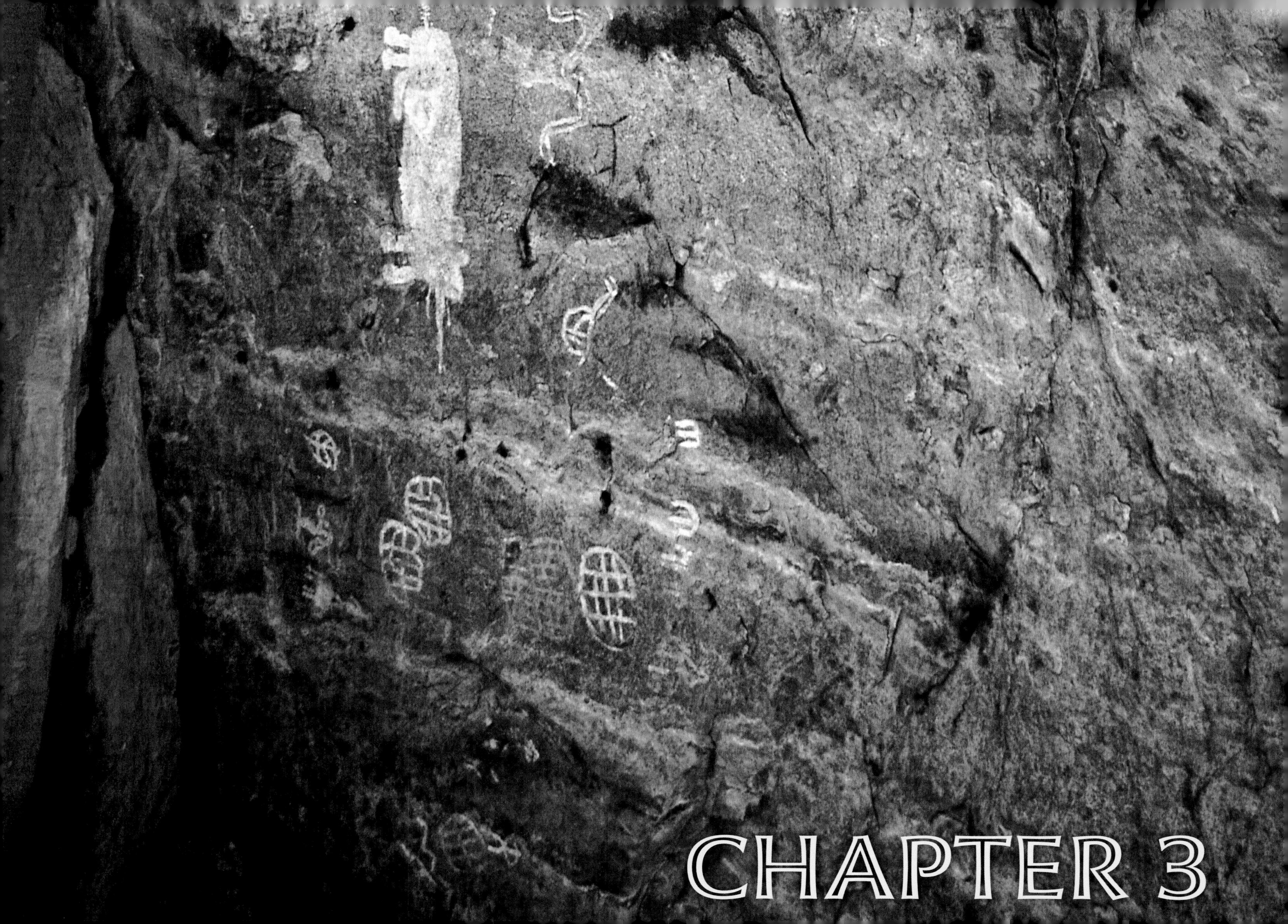
CHAPTER 3

Excavations of rock shelters tell us that people have been living at Tsodilo for at least one hundred thousand years. The Middle Stone Age peoples were among the earliest anatomically modern humans. The Later Stone Age peoples who followed them in southern Africa, as early as forty thousand years ago, most likely were the ancestors of the San.

Stone Age foragers lived by hunting and collecting wild foods. Later, after trading and interacting with food-producing people, they might adopt domesticated livestock, but primarily relied on game and forage. Living off livestock and crops is a very recent phenomenon. If the period of human occupation at Tsodilo were a clock where one hour represents the entire time span that people have been frequenting Tsodilo, during 59 minutes of that hour, people lived entirely from wild foods. It would only be during the last minute that they began to produce food for themselves.

What were these prehistoric inhabitants of Tsodilo like? How did they live? Three rock shelters offer us clues: White Paintings Shelter, Depression Shelter, and Rhino Cave.

A rock shelter is a natural cave-like outcrop that provides a relatively dry and protected area. The geological process of the formation of such shelters was described in chapter 2. Small groups of people briefly camped under the shelters during their seasonal rounds. All three of the shelters discussed in this chapter were painted, and so probably had ritual significance to their occupants. Their discarded broken and worn out tools, their accumulated food refuse, the charcoal from their cooking fires, and debris lay on the ground. Like people today, they also occasionally lost items such as small beads that slipped off necklaces or other items of clothing. Windblown sand and sediments buried the archaeological remains, layer after layer, waiting like keys to unlock an unknown world.

White Paintings Shelter

The most prominent rock shelter is also the most accessible, lying at the base of Male Hill. A painting of a large white bull elephant with its trunk and tail projecting straight out is featured prominently on the shelter wall. Surrounding it are geometric designs, along with animals and human figures with hands on their hips and some mounted on horses.

Fig. 3.1 (preceding page):
The white paintings that gave their name to White Paintings Shelter. Paintings include a large elephant, men mounted on horses, men with hands on hips, man holding a goat, a wheel, antelope, a snake, "m" shapes, geometric designs and a possible black horse facing left (above elephant). Samutjau explained that his ancestors and he himself as a young man used the shelter and white geometric painting at left to perform curing dance ceremonies.

Fig. 3.2 (right):
White Paintings Shelter where we excavated to a depth of seven meters and near the bottom recovered Middle Stone Age stone points close to a hundred thousand years old.

White Paintings Shelter contains the most extensive and complete record of the Tsodilo shelters. Excavating through layers seven meters deep, we find at the surface traces from occupation seventy years ago, to an estimated one hundred thousand years ago, at the bottom. Most deposits belong to the Later or Middle Stone Ages, separated by a substantial rock fall layer 4.2 meters beneath the surface. Occupation varied from short-term visits of a few weeks to use throughout much of the year, especially during the periods when intensive fishing was evident. Animal bones—which are abundant in the upper three meters, but poorly preserved below that depth—reveal over forty different species, including mammals, fish, reptiles, and birds. Some of the species of mammals found at the site are also depicted in the rock paintings (listed in **table 7.1**). Springhare, hare, and porcupine have at least a thirty-thousand-year record of use in the shelter, and, along with ostrich eggs and tortoise, constitute traditional foods of a diet still being exploited in the Kalahari today. Let us dig down into the past, outlining major characteristics from top to bottom of the excavations.

The upper 20 centimeters reveal evidence of maize, dried cow dung, small animal bones, ash deposits, and beads of glass, iron, and ostrich eggshell. The maize is quite recent. Yet here we also find Later Stone Age microlithic tools, small blades and points that were most likely hafted into wood and bone handles, or shafts (**figs. 3.3 & 3.4**). We find numerous mongongo nut shells, still a staple wild food resource at Tsodilo.

Microliths and pottery fragments are common between 20 centimeters and about 70 centimeters in Later Stone Age levels. Some potsherds had stamped and incised decoration similar to pottery found in the early villages of Divuyu and Nqoma, discussed in chapter 5, which suggests relationships between peoples of the villages and the rock shelter. In these layers we recovered delicate bone points that are identical to those used recently by traditional hunters in the Kalahari to tip arrows (**figs. 3.5 & 3.6**). With the exception of a 1,200-year-old domesticated sheep jaw, all bones were of wild animals.

Deposits from 80 to 130 centimeters revealed an extraordinary richness of fish bones, wetland animals, and broken barbed bone spear or harpoon points (**fig. 3.7**). More than two thousand fish bones were found from 110 to 120 centimeters alone, a level that dates to

Fig. 3.3 (*above*):
Stone blades and bladelets probably mounted in wooden or bone handles, excavated in White Paintings Shelter.

Fig. 3.4 (*above*):
Later Stone Age microliths also probably mounted for use and excavated in White Paintings Shelter.

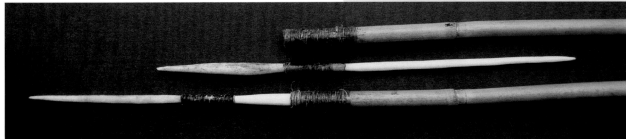

Figs. 3.5 (right) & 3.6 (below):
Comparison of prehistoric and modern bone arrow points and link-shafts. On the right, Later Stone Age bone points excavated in White Paintings Shelter. Below, modern bone points made in traditional fashion from giraffe tibia by Xauwe in about 2003.

between four thousand and seven thousand years ago. The fish included a large form of catfish as well as cichlids such as tilapia or bream.

As mentioned previously, the barbed bone points had not previously been found in southern Africa. The closest similar finds were far to the north in eastern Congo and at Lake Turkana in Kenya, along the Nile and in the Sahara. The sheer quantity of fish bones, and the discarded broken fish spear points found at the site, almost certainly indicate that fish were obtained near the site. The fish were probably speared or harpooned in shallow water during spawning runs up nearby rivers that no longer flow; or at the Tsodilo Lake. The nearest fishing at present requires a long trek to the Okavango River.

Fig. 3.7 (above):
Broken bone harpoon or spear points excavated in layers of sediment containing hundreds of fish bones.

Figs. 3.8 (above) & 3.9 (right):
Compare the geometric designs. Above, a decorated bone artifact excavated in the 110- to 120-centimeter level in White Paintings Shelter and dated to about four thousand five hundred years ago; and on the right, the geometric rock painting (see also Fig. 7.1).

Along with river fish the deposits also revealed the presence of wetland animals—vlei rat, bushpig, lechwe, and reedbuck—along with springhare, tortoise, monitor lizard, zebra, eland, rhinoceros, and buffalo. There were numerous grindstones and the occasional carbonized mongongo nutshell fragment. A truly unique find was a delicately engraved bone ornament, or point, marked by a design that resembles a fish spine or plant (figs. 3.8 & 3.9).

The Oldest Ostrich Eggshell Beads

Descending from 140 to 210 centimeters, artifacts and bones grew scarcer, while broken ostrich eggshells grew abundant. Most of the shell fragments were not worked, so it may be that the eggs were primarily collected for food. However, some were used for making beads, which proved very significant due to the beads' age. Ostrich eggshell beads are found at Later Stone Age sites throughout much of eastern and southern Africa, including the Kalahari, where they are still made and sold as traditional craft items (**figs. 10.3 & 10.6**).

Indeed, the Tsodilo excavations revealed one of the most continuous records of bead making in the world. At White Paintings Shelter beads and unfinished specimens were found in almost every level from the surface to two meters deep—that is, from the twentieth century down through much of the Later Stone Age. None were found in the Middle Stone Age deposits. The 190- to 200-centimeter level turned up a bead and bead fragment with a drilled hole. This fragment was radiocarbon dated to between twenty-six and twenty-seven thousand years ago, one of the oldest directly dated ostrich eggshell beads so far found in Africa.

More Evidence of Fishing

The layers at 210 to 280 centimeters uncovered another series of Later Stone Age levels rich in fish bones (again large catfish and bream), as well as a freshwater mollusk shell dated to between thirty-three and thirty-four thousand years ago. Beyond fish, bone remains show occupants of the rock shelter hunted a wide variety of mammals, from wetland species like bushbuck and reedbuck, to rock-jumping klipspringer (a small antelope), to the now extinct giant Cape zebra. No plant foods survived from this period, but a broad-spectrum diet was evident.

These lower, fish-rich levels reveal numerous Later Stone Age microlithic artifacts. People produced small blades and carefully blunted the backs of some of them. Archaeologists reason that some of these backed tools were attached to wood shafts and used as arrow barbs. If true, then use of the bow and arrow is very old at Tsodilo. Several bone points were also found in these levels. One is quite sharp and could easily have tipped a fish spear; other fragments were barbed. Finally, a most unusual broken bone point was reconstructed in the lab from three pieces. The thin point was marked by at least thirty-six circular incisions of unknown purpose.

Fig. 3.10 (left):
Children using baskets to catch small fish on the floodplains near Tamatshaa. The baskets are laid in a row. The children walk towards them beating the water, driving fish into the baskets which are then upended. This method of fishing could date back to the times when Tsodilo people were leaving fish bones in their middens.

Below the levels with abundant fish bones, sediment analysis showed evidence of a substantial dry period. Artifacts and bones grew scarce while microliths gave way to large blades, along with bone fragments of a now extinct large form of hartebeest or tsessebe.

The Middle Stone Age

At one stage, 410 to 420 centimeters below the surface, rocks fell from the roof of the shelter. This rock fall layer caps the Middle Stone Age deposits, best recognized by their distinctive stone spear points. Indeed, Middle Stone Age points like those found at this site are among the oldest clearly recognizable spear points known in Africa **(fig. 3.11)**.

The Middle Stone Age represents the oldest period of human occupation that has thus far been uncovered at Tsodilo—a thermoluminescence age of 94,300 years ago—from a sample of sand excavated at a depth of 605 centimeters. This method of dating measures the last time the sand was exposed to sunlight when it was part of the ground surface. It is reasonable to think that the underlying deposits are likely to be at least one hundred thousand years old. Another thermoluminescence date of 66,400 years ago was obtained on sand from a depth of 500 centimeters. Overall, these dates imply that the Middle Stone Age occupation at Tsodilo lasted for at least thirty thousand years.

Fig. 3.11 (above):
Middle Stone Age stone points possibly mounted
for use as spear points.

Abundant evidence for stone tool manufacture during the Middle Stone Age includes hundreds of waste flakes recovered along with numerous cores that were used to produce them. Middle Stone Age peoples at both White Paintings Shelter and Rhino Cave used quartz, a rock that is plentiful at Tsodilo. Yet they preferred to use nonlocal, flintlike rocks for making points and other finished tools. Such rocks included silcrete, commonly found at pans and along river valleys, as well as several colorful varieties of chert, chalcedony, and jasper. To get these rocks people had to either travel considerable distances from Tsodilo or trade for them through a raw material exchange network in the general area, which implies that Middle Stone Age people had a sophisticated knowledge of the region and were not restricted in their movements.

The Depression Shelter

Located on Female Hill, the Depression site—named after the large numbers of rock indentations, or cupules **(fig. 4.1)**, explored in chapter 4—consists of a natural rock overhang, a cave-like fissure that is also partially protected by an overhang and an open area in front **(fig. 3.12)**. Excavations in this area exposed 5.1 meters of deposits and show a record of occupation spanning forty thousand years. Yet in many ways these layers reveal as much through what they lack as through what they contain.

Fig. 3.12 (above):
*Depression Shelter. The wall of cupules (**fig. 4.1**) is visible behind the twisted tree. The main excavation was conducted outside the shelter with a one square meter pit sunk below the visible cupules.*

Again we find refuse from eaten animals. Almost all of the bones—springhare, hare, warthog, steenbok, gray duiker, and tortoise—were concentrated in the upper meter near the shelter wall. Yet unlike at White Paintings Shelter, no fish bones or barbed bone points were found. Such differences in findings at nearby sites underscore the value of having a knowledge of more than one site in order to obtain a more complete understanding of the past.

Let's peel back the layers once again. Surface excavations down to 20 centimeters revealed Later Stone Age microlithic tools such as small scrapers, backed segments or crescents, and a few glass beads of European origin, implying a relatively recent age for these deposits.

The next 30 centimeters proved rich in Later Stone Age tools, with an abundance of flaking debris, along with small scrapers, backed crescents, and small double-backed drills. Thumbnail-sized scrapers have convex edges; they were almost certainly hafted to a wooden or bone handle. Microscopic study of the working edges shows scrapers were used either on hide or on wood, while the drills bored into a hard substance, such as ostrich eggshell. The presence of so many worn out and discarded small scrapers means that hide scraping and/or wood working were important activities. The discovery of potsherds with stamped and incised decoration similar to pottery found at the nearby villages of Nqoma and Divuyu suggests an age of between 1,000 and 1,500 years ago. These levels also yielded several small iron wrist guard clips, identical to those found at the villages. Interestingly, such clips were not found in the corresponding deposits at White Paintings Shelter, nor were there many of the small scrapers or double-backed drills at that site. The differences in stone artifacts at the two sites hint that different activities were being carried out at each shelter during the same general period.

The number of stone artifacts drops off substantially in deposits below 60 centimeters, or roughly two thousand years ago, signaling the period before the knowledge of metallurgy and pottery at Tsodilo. This indicates a very long period when Later Stone Age people used the site, between approximately two thousand and ten thousand years ago. During this time people used the site frequently, but for short periods. To sift the increasingly scarce evidence, archaeologists screened with a mosquito net lining the sieve. What emerged? Two very small fragments of mongongo nutshell—the Kalahari's oldest known wild plant food—from the 140- to 150-centimeter level dated to about eight thousand years ago.

The deposits from the last part of the Pleistocene, or Ice Age, situated between 200 and 325 centimeters, span from fifteen thousand to about twenty-six thousand years ago, a period of increased rainfall. Only a few stone artifacts were found, suggesting intermittent use of the site. Deposits below 400 centimeters, or at about thirty thousand years ago, turned up many more artifacts, suggesting more intensive use of the site. The tool makers' preference for quartz over silcrete and chert at this site could mean that people were either trading less or not venturing far from Tsodilo **(fig. 3.14)**. One interesting find was a small piece of ground chromite from the 480- to 500-centimeter level (about forty thousand years ago), likely used to produce pigment. This find tells us that decorative coloring, perhaps for body paint, has a very long history at Tsodilo.

Fig. 3.13 (above):
Samutjau and Larry screening "dirt"
while Wright Kgosietsile stands in
the main excavation. Below
upper levels, the sand turned
a wonderful orange color.

Fig. 3.14 (above):
Quartz point excavated in the 440- to 460-centimeter level. The point, mounted by us for illustrative purposes, probably dates between thirty-five and forty thousand years ago.

Fig. 3.15 (right):
*Excavation in Rhino Shelter. George Brook (in pit) taking soil samples for dating purposes. The rhino painting (**figs. 3.16 & 3.17**) is above the screen on the right wall. Controversy among archaeologists has been stirred by the suggestion that the shape on the left wall above the stones (**fig. 3.18**) is actually a carved snake created for ritual purposes.*

Rhino Cave

On the wall of a small, naturally hidden site located on Female Hill stands an impressive white painting of a large rhinoceros or possibly an elephant that has been painted over a red giraffe, set among other faded red geometric designs (**figs. 3.16 & 3.17**). The opposite wall contains more than three hundred depressions and grooves (**fig. 3.18**), discussed in detail in the next chapter. We were the first archaeologists to excavate this site, in 1995, and during our pioneering work we noticed the unusual patterns of sunlight that illuminated the wall with the depressions during late July. Recent radiocarbon dating of naturally deposited organic material extracted from one of the depressions has indicated that this particular depression must have been ground at least 6,000 years ago. However, other depressions at this site could be more recent. The impressive paintings and wall with depressions in this comparatively small cave suggest that the site may have been used for ritual purposes. Excavations beneath the paintings dug approximately 150 centimeters down recovered more than fourteen thousand stone artifacts, primarily flaking debris, that belong to the Later or Middle Stone Ages. Yet the deposits in the upper 20 to 25 centimeters contained a few charcoal-tempered, fingernail-decorated potsherds that reveal that Rhino Cave was being visited between 1,600 and 1,700 years ago. Later Stone Age deposits excavated between 70 and 75 centimeters were dated to a little older than 5,000 years ago.

As at Depression and White Paintings Shelter, mongongo nutshell fragments were common finds at Rhino Cave above 50 centimeters. Unlike the Depression site and White Paintings Shelter, no ostrich eggshell, iron, or glass beads were found in our excavations here. Bones were rare and those few that were found did not include fish.

Figs. 3.16 (above) & 3.17 (below):
The rhino or elephant painting in Rhino Cave. A water seep bifurcates the rhino exposing earlier red paintings of a giraffe and geometric design. Red circles, one containing a grid (see below), are visible behind the rhino while a faded red image, possibly an animal, faces the rhino.

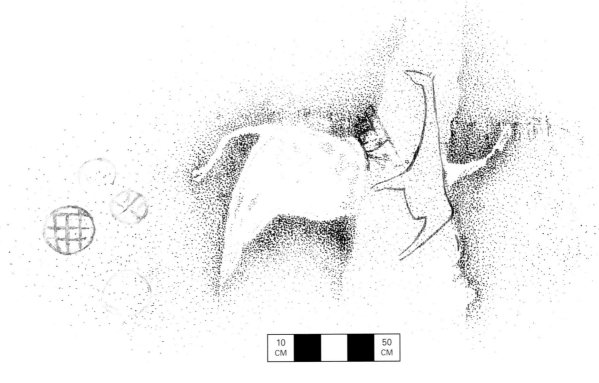

10 CM			50 CM

Fig. 3.18 (above):
The carved shape on the left wall of Rhino Shelter that has created controversy by being described as a "snake."

Indeed, in the lower layers we recovered one hundred Middle Stone Age points, including unfinished specimens, broken tips, and bases **(fig. 3.19)**. Rich concentrations of flaking debris and hammer stones show Rhino Cave was a location where early people produced tools. Since most debris fell near a large boulder, that may well have served as a seat for ancient stone workers. The Middle Stone Age points showed considerable care and skill, and many were made through the same method: the flake used to produce the point had the striking platform (the impact area where the flake was struck from the core) on the corner of the base of the point. The fact that the points were being made in this fashion throughout the Middle Stone Age levels at Rhino Cave reveals that a specific manufacturing tradition was learned and maintained over a considerable period.

The Middle Stone Age folk at Rhino Cave also made scrapers by splitting small cores in order to utilize the thick flakes for making a convex scraping edge. No such scrapers appear in the Middle Stone Age levels at White Paintings Shelter. However, at both Rhino Cave and White Paintings Shelter nonlocal rocks such as silcrete and various cherts were preferred for making finished tools such as points. Finally, one unique artifact found in the Middle Stone Age deposits at Rhino Cave is a thin slab of specularite or hematite. The slab, which has a convex edge, has been polished by intensive rubbing, perhaps in preparing hides, or for the production of pigment. The use of pigment by Middle Stone Age peoples was widespread in southern Africa, but there is no evidence for rock shelter paintings during this period.

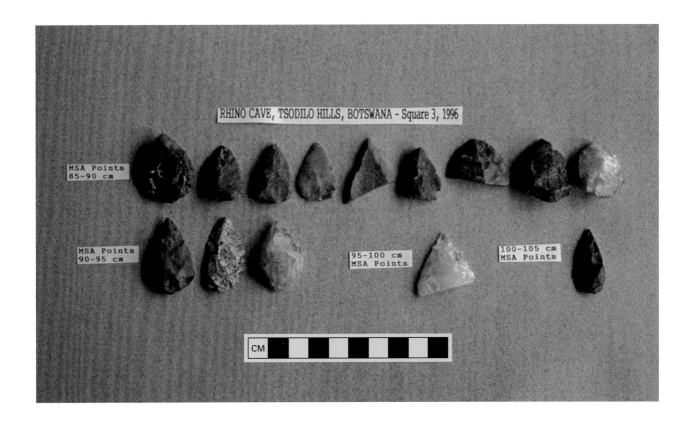

Fig. 3.19 (above):
Middle Stone Age points excavated in Rhino Cave.

Conclusion

Taken together, the three rock shelters unlock windows into our past, revealing the long record of human occupation at Tsodilo. We have not indisputably identified the first people of Tsodilo, but we know they arrived here at least one hundred thousand years ago, and judging from finds made elsewhere, were anatomically modern humans. Middle Stone Age hunter-foragers can be identified from their finely crafted stone spear points found at Rhino Cave and White Paintings Shelter. The latter site served as a periodic base camp from which people would hunt wild game, fish and gather plant foods as part of seasonal activities.

Tools changed by the beginning of the Later Stone Age; stone spear points were replaced by small, microlithic, crescent-shaped blades and bone points, some of which bear a striking resemblance to those used to tip arrows in the Kalahari's recent historic era.

Yet the most important, exciting, and surprising artifacts were the skillfully fashioned barbed bone points that tipped fish spears, or harpoons, which had never before been found in southern Africa. Combined with the hundreds of fish bones at White Paintings Shelter, history books will now have to rank fishing (of large catfish and bream) along with hunting (everything from rodents to rhinos) and gathering (tortoise, ostrich eggs, and mongongo nuts) as an integral part of prehistoric subsistence at this place in the not always so "dry" Kalahari.

We also discovered that the manufacture of ostrich eggshell beads goes back at least twenty-seven thousand years and the use of pigment dates back to a minimum of forty thousand years ago. Perhaps the wearing of beads was as an expression of personal beauty, or group identity, or both. There are no absolute answers, only more provocative questions. Yet each of these findings reaches out to us from the dust and decay of the shelters as a message from the past. ■

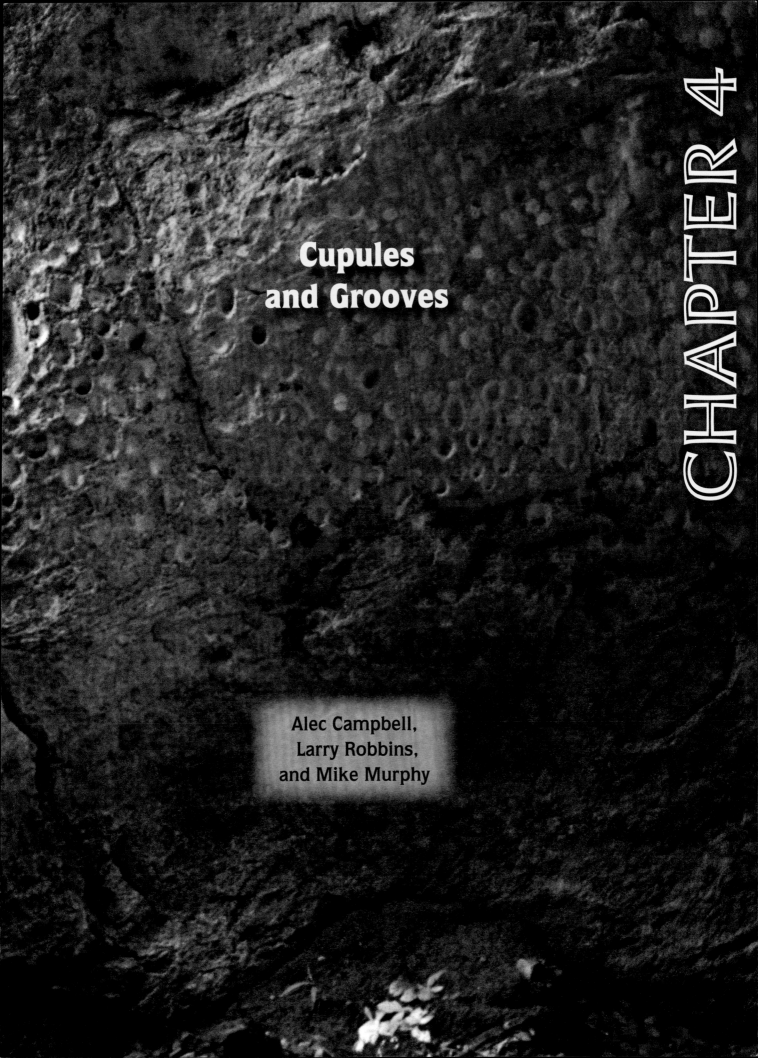

Cupules
and Grooves

CHAPTER 4

Alec Campbell,
Larry Robbins,
and Mike Murphy

There are no rock engravings at Tsodilo depicting, as the paintings do, people, geometric designs, or animals. Yet there are small depressions known as cupules and various shaped grooves that have been chipped and ground into the rock at more than twenty-five sites.

Most of these occur at sites on Female Hill, although there are at least four places where they occur on Male Hill, and there is one site found by Nick Walker on Child Hill. Grooves are usually easy to see, but cupules can be eroded or have a patina similar to surrounding rock surfaces and as a result be difficult to recognize. Almost certainly, more sites remain to be located.

Cupules

Cupules, also termed "cup-marks," are saucer-shaped indentations hammered and ground into the rock face. They can occur at places that also have paintings, and sometimes alone. Average cupules are about 5 centimeters or more wide and less than 1 centimeter deep, although a few are very much larger, one being approximately 12 centimeters wide and 9 centimeters deep. There are a very few single isolated cupules; but, for the most part, they are found in groups ranging from five to one hundred or, in three cases, considerably more. There are 346 cupules, or rather carved shapes, on a vertical wall in Rhino Cave (figs. 3.18 & 4.4),

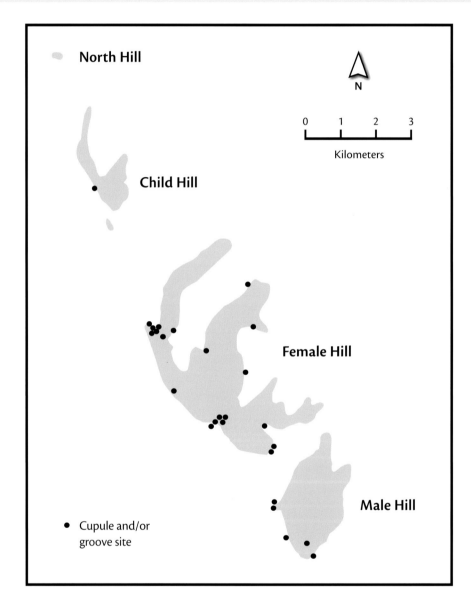

Map 4.1 (above):
Distribution of cupule and groove sites across Tsodilo Hills.

Fig. 4.1 (preceding page):
Some one thousand one hundred cupules adorn one rock wall in Depression Shelter.

and nearly 1,100 cupules on a wall in Depression Shelter (**fig. 4.1**) and more than one hundred cupules in Corner Cave (**fig. 4.2**), but these are exceptional places. Most of the Tsodilo cupules have been ground into vertical or near-vertical walls, although a very few are on horizontal surfaces; for instance, in the cave at the south end of Female Hill. Some cupules are heavily patinated and almost invisible, while others, such as some of those in Rhino Cave, look so fresh that they could have been made yesterday.

There are also cupules next to dormant springs that very occasionally emit water. Two of these are beside the path that climbs into Gubekho Gorge; another place is next to Tshokgam (Python Spring or Water Hole Mine); and yet another such place is beside a shallow fissure at the base of Male Hill. In addition, cupules are located in four caves, three of which also contain paintings. Cupules leading down to White Rhino Shelter, a cave in a low rocky finger projecting from the east base of Female Hill that also contains paintings and another group of cupules ground into the vertical lower rock face, are now almost hidden by a fallen slab that leans against the wall, only a few centimeters away from them.

Single large cupules are found on two freestanding rocks that may mark rock gongs. One occurs on a rock near the spring in upper Gubekho Gorge, and another is in the cave above the main cave with cupules at the south end of

Fig. 4.2 (above):
Cupules ground into a ledge in Corner Cave. A broken round quartz spheroid, found near the cave, lies in a cupule at bottom right.

Female Hill. Such large rocks are widely distributed in Africa and they resonate, or produce unusual sounds, when struck with a stone. Otherwise, the purposes of the cupules remain uncertain, although we can make guesses as to what some of these may have been. Hambukushu have suggested that they were used for cracking nuts, but this is unlikely because most of them are found on vertical surfaces.

A number of round, ground quartz artifacts shaped like balls were excavated in Kudu Horn Shelter, just north of White Paintings Shelter, in levels that may date to about two thousand years ago. Archaeologists have sometimes termed these balls "spheroids." This shelter has no paintings but does have some fifty cupules ground into its back wall not far from where the stone balls were found. Only a few meters from Kudu Horn Shelter, cupules occur on a flat loose rock in the passageway entering Ancestors' Cave. Just inside the cave, more cupules occur on a sloping ledge. Perhaps the cupules on the loose rock, as Nick Walker has pointed out, marked a place where prayers had to be said before entering the cave, or beyond which only initiates might proceed.

Similar quartz balls, or spheroids, were also recovered in the excavations of outlying test squares at White Paintings Shelter in 1993. They were found in Later Stone Age deposits. In contrast to Kudu Horn Shelter, they were not found immediately adjacent to a wall with cupules. A further broken quartz ball was found wedged between rocks just outside Corner Cave. These quartz balls, somewhat smaller than tennis balls, fit fairly neatly into some of the cupules and may have been the means of the cupules' final grinding (fig. 4.2). Even so, we do not know for what reason the cupules were made. Obviously, they provided a symbol on the rock that may have meant something to those who made them. Perhaps they were a statement about the place where they occur or a way to denote the number of visits an individual or group made to the site. Maybe their makers may have taken ground powder from the cupule or used the quartz ball for purposes of their own.

Grooves

Grooves, which are less common than cupules, but often more visible, have also been ground into the rock. They have smooth surfaces and usually occur in small groups ranging from three to fifteen. They are roughly "canoe-shaped," rarely more than twenty centimeters long and three centimeters wide, and vary in depth between three and ten millimeters. Grooves have been found only on horizontal or near-horizontal surfaces, on upper surfaces of freestanding rocks, on pavements, and in shelters. Grooves appear to be considerably more recent in age than most cupules.

In addition to the wall of cupules, Depression Shelter has two sets of grooves, one on a nearly-buried rock at the foot of fallen boulders at the back of the shelter, and the other on the top of those fallen boulders. There are also four small grooves on a low rock in the valley floor at the foot of Gubekho Gorge. A similar set of grooves has been ground into a rock on the floor of the valley entrance near the Rhino Panel. Grooves also appear at the entrance to the valley leading up to the Sex Site.

Other sets of grooves occur on rocks at sites that also contain rock paintings. These sites include: Handprint Shelter on the Divuyu Trail, Crab Shelter on Cliff Trail (fig. 4.3), and a remote shelter at the north of Female Hill.

As with the cupules, the purposes for which the grooves were made are unknown. Their somewhat rounded rather than "pinched" bottoms suggest that they were not used for sharpening metal tools. Their groupings and positions also suggest they were not necessarily used for grinding substances such as ocher or seeds. A thin slab of stone with a curved ground edge was excavated at some depth in Depression Shelter and fitted neatly into one of the same shelter's grooves.

Fig. 4.3 (left):
A pattern of grooves on the floor of Crab Shelter. Large pieces of laterite were also found in the shelter. More laterite lay outside the shelter, some of it burned possibly to make red pigment.

Rhino Cave

In chapter 3, we note how, in Rhino Cave in 1995 we saw some of the cupules and ground shapes on the south wall light up when the late afternoon sun shone onto them through a hole at the western end of the shelter. At the time of our pioneering work at this site we noted that those who made the ground shapes must have been aware of this phenomenon and that perhaps such illumination held meaning for them.

In late 2006, Rhino Cave was brought sharply to public attention by press releases and stories appearing on the web. One document, for instance, appearing on NationalGeographic.com read: "'Python Cave' Reveals Oldest Human Ritual, Scientists Suggest," and another, on Scientific American.com (www.sciam.com), noted: "70,000-year old African ritual practices linked to mythology of modern Batswanans."

The proposal that the carved cave wall could represent a snake, first put forward by Nick Walker and later publicized by Sheila Coulson, is controversial, to say the least. Sitting at the northeast corner of the cave and looking along the south wall, the engravings could resemble the head and body of an approaching scaled snake. Yet this may easily be fortuitous, since there is little doubt that the carvings on the wall were made during different ages. Nor does the panel when viewed directly resemble a snake. In addition, the shapes are not carved in any regular manner, as they comprise cupules, ovals, short and long grooves, and even teardrops **(fig. 4.4)**. Walker and Coulson also point to a concealed crevice behind the carved panel in which a person can stand and speak without being visible, suggesting to viewers that the snake speaks.

Fig. 4.4 (above):
A section of the wall carvings in Rhino Cave. Shapes include cupules, ovals, short and long grooves and even teardrops. Nor do the carvings appear to have been made at the same time. Some of those on the left have a silica coating while some on the right are so fresh that a licked finger brings away ground dust. George Brook has obtained a minimum date for one carving of over five thousand years.

On the opposite wall are paintings, a large white rhinoceros or elephant bifurcated by a water seep exposing an earlier red finger-painting of a giraffe and red geometric pattern (**figs. 3.16 & 3.17**). Beside the rhino are faded but very visible geometric designs, including a number of red circles containing grids. Coulson has used the rhino and giraffe paintings, which cannot be more than two thousand years old (the giraffe is painted in the same style as Tsodilo's numerous red paintings of cattle), to suggest that the so-called snake represents a seventy-thousand-year-old ancestor of modern San beliefs. The *National Geographic* news release has added to the confusion by stating that, "rituals like those Coulson describes are depicted in ancient paintings throughout the Tsodilo Hills ..." This is absolutely untrue: there are only two known paintings of snakes at Tsodilo and neither of these, nor any other paintings, depict rituals involving hidden people giving voice to snakes.

In addition, it is currently impossible to directly date the ground shapes that make up the "snake." Some of these grindings may be old, even seventy thousand years old; but evidence of this age is needed. One of the cupules at Rhino Cave has been investigated by George Brook by sampling and radiocarbon dating organic matter extracted from the surface of the cupule. As mentioned previously, the resulting date is over five thousand years ago, providing a minimum age for that cupule, but it does not tell us when the cupule was actually ground. The presumed seventy-thousand-year-old date mentioned above is based on comparing Middle Stone Age artifacts found in the deposits with the ages of similar artifacts found at White Paintings Shelter and at the site of Gci, located in the Kalahari to the southwest of Tsodilo.

Many of the other shapes and cupules look very recent, and a finger rubbed along their surfaces comes away with rock dust on it.

A World Perspective

Both grooves and cupules are common, not only throughout Africa, but also in Europe, Asia, Australasia, and the Americas. At Chifubwa Stream in Zambia, Desmond Clark has dated cupules to about 6,300 years ago. In India, Robert Bednarik dated cupules to the Lower Palaeolithic, or Early Stone Age, while others from La Ferrassie in France are known from a Neanderthal burial dating to the Middle Palaeolithic. Recently, Leore Grossman and Naama Goren-Inbar have shown that Neolithic examples found at a site in Israel resulted from extracting flint nodules from the rock. However, this was not the case for Tsodilo, where there is no evidence for the extraction of nodules from within the cupules. Other examples, such as those found ground into the horizontal surface of boulders in California, were most likely used for processing nuts. It is clear that cupules span an immense period of time, and it also seems that their function varied considerably.

There is absolutely no reason to believe that cupules at Tsodilo are necessarily contemporaneous with the rock paintings. Some may have the same age as the paintings, but others, from their patina and general wear, are probably much older, possibly dating as far back as the Middle Stone Age. Of course, there may have been paintings on the rocks at times when the earliest cupules were made but, if such paintings existed, they have long since disappeared.

Cupules and grooves are often overlooked at Tsodilo in favor of the paintings but, considering their possible age, potential scientific significance, and large number, are well worth noting. ■

Nqoma   Divuyu

Early Villages at Tsodilo:
The Introduction of Livestock,
Crops, and Metalworking

CHAPTER 5

Edwin N. Wilmsen
and James R. Denbow

Just after the beginning of the second half of the first millennium AD, peoples bringing new technologies and economies began to build stable villages on the Divuyu and Nqoma plateaus at Tsodilo.

Before this, some presumably Khoesan-speaking people around the margins of the Okavango had added pottery making and cattle to a broad spectrum foraging economy. While these changes were occurring, people continued to rely upon stone tools identical to those found at earlier Later Stone Age sites throughout the northern Kalahari. By the eighth century the pace of change in technology, subsistence, and settlement increased as iron and copper metallurgy was introduced and cultivated cereal crops were added to the economy. Sheep and goats augmented the small numbers of domestic cattle kept by some earlier communities, and the construction of pole-and-daga houses in well-defined villages is evident for the first time. Elaborately finished and decorated pottery vessels were used for cooking, storing, and serving food. People were also elaborately adorned with chains and bangles of copper and iron, ostrich eggshell, and glass beads, along with ivory bracelets and other jewelry. The quantity and variety of these luxury goods at Tsodilo suggest that among these people were some who were wealthy and powerful for their time. These rapid changes suggest that many of these new villages incorporated within them Bantu-speaking peoples in the process of expanding southward along the river systems from the Congo through Angola and Central Africa. The Divuyu and Nqoma settlements in the Tsodilo Hills, along with Xaro and Matlapaneng on the Delta (see **map 0.1**), are the earliest such villages discovered and excavated in the western half of southern Africa.

The Villages in Space and Time

The Hills lie in the midst of the northern Kalahari dunefield, during the building of which sand piled up on the eastern sides of the Hills. This had a consequence critical for human occupation of the Female Hill: the eastward dip of the rocks allowed sand to be blown higher up the slope, forming a sand ramp that greatly facilitates access to its upper areas. Also, in the dune

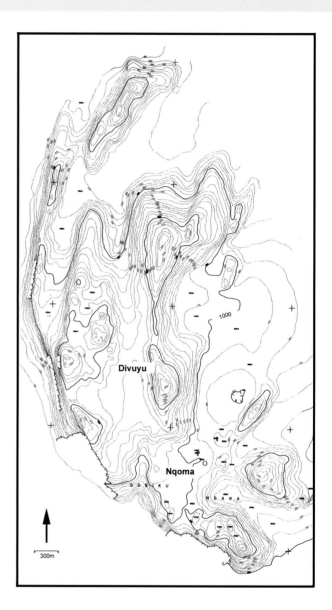

Map 5.1 (above):
Map of Female Hill indicating Divuyu and Nqoma plateaus.

Fig. 5.1 (preceding page):
Female Hill rising above the plain as seen from the top of Male Hill. The Divuyu and Nqoma plateaus can be clearly discerned as can the rock ramparts on the east and west sides of Divuyu. The two eastern sand-ramp approaches to Nqoma are also visible.

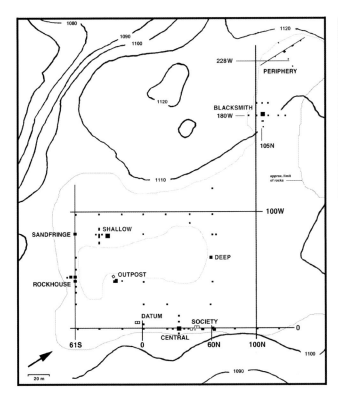

Fig. 5.2 (*above*):
Standing on the southern end of the Divuyu plateau, looking down on Nqoma. Male Hill rises in the background.

Map 5.2 (*left*):
Nqoma excavation plan.

building process the irregular rock substrate of the plateaus filled in and leveled, forming the only flat habitable areas on the Hills (**fig. 5.1 & map 5.1**). Nqoma, the lower and smaller plateau (**fig. 5.2**), lies 90 meters above the surrounding plain. The only practicable access to it is up this broad, gently sloping ramp of sand that is easily passable by people and livestock. About 70 meters higher, the Divuyu plateau abuts Nqoma at the juncture where the sand ramp merges into the latter plateau. It is ringed by rocky prominences that drop precipitously 160 meters from the level of the plateau to the calcrete flats (**fig. 5.3**). Thus, the only practical route to Divuyu for people with domestic animals is via the sand ramp to Nqoma and then up a moderately steep ridge at the northern end of the lower plateau. This has important implications for social relations during the simultaneous occupation of the two sites throughout much of the eighth and ninth centuries.

The Nqoma plateau was first settled by small groups in its northwest and southwest corners. We do

Fig. 5.3 (*above*):
The Divuyu plateau seen from the western rock rampart. The baobab after which the site was named is marked ("Divuyu" means "Place of the Baobab" in Tjimbukushu). The rock shelter to the left of the red arrow contains several rock paintings. Male Hill is visible at back right.

Map 5.3 (*right*):
Divuyu excavation plan.

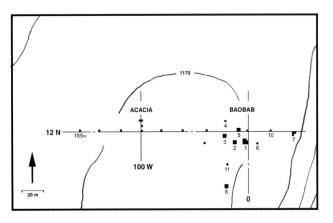

not know exactly when this took place, but it must have begun a considerable time before intensive settlement of both the Nqoma and Divuyu plateaus occurred around AD 650. In some parts of the site, particularly those areas labeled as Blacksmith in the northwest corner and Sandfringe in the southwest, the cultural stratigraphy extended below the main occupation to include strata where large numbers of stone artifacts, but few ceramics, were recovered (**maps 5.2 & 5.3**). On present evidence, the Divuyu plateau was not occupied at this time. Subsequently, after about AD 650 residential areas were established on both plateaus; these Nqoma and Divuyu settlements were initially of roughly the same size, suggesting that comparable social units resided at each. However, some prominent dissimilarities set the two sites clearly apart. The first notable difference is that the Divuyu plateau was probably occupied for no more than 125 years—but possibly as late as AD 875—while the Nqoma plateau continued to be settled, although perhaps intermittently, well into the nineteenth century.

Material Life

Pottery

There is little discernable change in ceramic design motifs throughout the settlement of Divuyu (**fig. 5.4**); these may be bracketed into three broadly defined categories. Most numerous are thick bowls and jars with several bands parallel to the rim that are commonly filled with alternating bands of incised and comb-stamped hatching, sometimes alternating with unfilled bands. Most of these vessels contain inclusions of diatoms along with charcoal and show evidence they were heated to high temperatures, perhaps during use as cooking pots. The alternating decoration techniques and use of unfilled bands make these vessels stylistically similar to sherds dating to the third and fourth centuries AD found along the Loango coast of the Republic of Congo.

Fig. 5.4 (above):
Divuyu sherds.

The second category is of thin-walled bowls and jars, often without inflection of the neck or rim. Two distinct motif sets are associated with this category; the first consists of single or double lines of punctates or fingernail impressions parallel to and just below the rim, the lip of which is sometimes also decorated with incised lines or punctates. The second motif set consists of interlocking triangles, merging into rhomboids, filled with incised lines on the upper half of vessels. At Xaro on the Okavango River this thin-walled category is predominant, with by far the majority of sherds displaying variations of punctate line motifs.

A third category consists of a handful of bowls that are decorated with incised lines in sub-triangular areas below raised rims similar to designs on many Nqoma sherds. These are the only vessels at Divuyu on which a red hematite slip had been applied. This, and their decoration motifs, suggests they were not made at

the site but imported from elsewhere. Such serving vessels are found in contemporary levels at Nqoma where they predominate during the peak of its settlement between about AD 900 and 1100.

Nqoma presents a more complex picture. In the earliest levels prior to about AD 900, sherds are in part similar to those of Divuyu (**fig. 5.5**); there are, however, two other distinct sets of sherds that are either earlier or perhaps contemporary with Divuyu. The first closely resembles some contemporary counterparts at Matlapaneng on the southeastern edge of the Delta. These sherds are from bag-shaped vessels with densely spaced parallel lines of comb stamping, occasionally interspersed with a row of false-relief chevrons, covering most of the vessel body (**fig. 5.6**). Such vessels are unknown at Divuyu. The second (**fig. 5.7**) is thin-walled with a hard

Fig. 5.5 (above):
Nqoma sherds with Divuyu affinities.

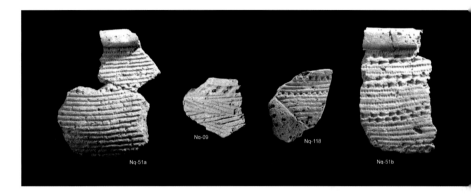

Fig. 5.6 (above):
Matlapaneng sherds.

paste and a variety of design techniques employing incised surface patterns, including what may be cord-rolled surface texturing overdrawn with finely incised curvilinear motifs; many of these vessels had a red slip. Following this, from about AD 900 to AD 1200, collared, thickened-rim jars and small serving bowls associated with the traditions of the Victoria Falls and northern Zambezi regions of Zambia are the most common in all parts of the site; these also make up the majority of the ceramic assemblage at Matlapaneng and must reflect a significant influx of peoples from the Zambezi region. While collared jars for cooking and storage make up about 20 percent of the Nqoma assemblage, the majority (80 percent) of the vessels were small bowls, many of a shallow

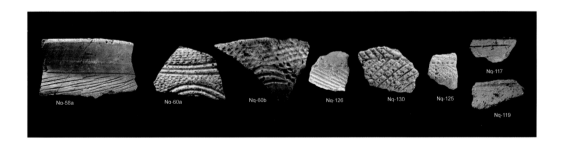

Fig. 5.7 (left):
Pre-AD 900 sherds.

dishlike or carinated form with capacities of about a half liter. Almost all were covered with a red ocher slip. With few exceptions, these bowls were elaborately decorated (**fig. 5.8**), usually with triangles pendant from the body-rim inflection or with interlocking triangles around the shoulder that were filled with incised or comb-stamped lines often bounded at the neck junction by punctates or false-relief chevrons. In the early part of this period, most bowls had rounder shoulders with somewhat concave, slightly everted rims. This shape evolved later into vessels with more sharply carinated shoulders and high, flaring, everted rims. By the end of this "evolved" period, half the interior depth of some bowls was formed by the height of the rim. After the thirteenth century, some

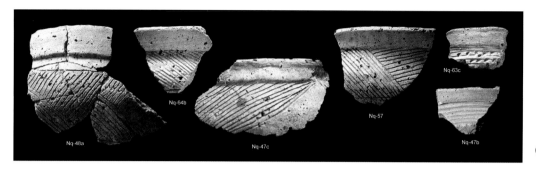

Fig. 5.8 (left):
Classic Nqoma sherds.

vessel shapes and decoration styles that had appeared earlier **(fig. 5.9)** continued to be made and may have been ancestral to early Hambukushu wares, which appear sometime around the sixteenth or seventeenth century **(fig. 5.10)** at Nqoma and are radiocarbon dated at Xaro on the Delta to this time range.

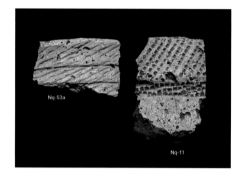

Fig. 5.9 (left):
Twelfth-to-thirteenth-century
Nqoma sherds.

Fig. 5.10 (right):
Proto-Hambukushu
Nqoma sherds.

Iron and Copper

Only two stone tools and a few flakes have been found at Divuyu; this low incidence, plus a comparable paucity at the related Delta site, Xaro, strongly imply that the people who lived in these communities did not use stone tools. Rather, it would seem those found were lost there by stone-using visitors who lived nearby, perhaps at Nqoma, where stone implements and fabrication debris are common. The greatest concentrations of this material occur in the southwestern and northwestern corners of Nqoma at Sandfringe and Blacksmith, which predate AD 750 —perhaps by several centuries. Others occur in strata contemporary with Divuyu. These stone implements were made of a variety of cherts, which had to be imported, some perhaps from honey-colored chert outcrops located near Shakawe on the Delta. Stone tools remained in use at Nqoma in variable but significant numbers throughout the 1,200 years of its occupation. They again became abundant, for instance, in the upper levels of the Blacksmith location, where they are associated with European materials.

Although metal was introduced to the Hills by people who settled at Divuyu, metal artifacts are relatively uncommon at the site; iron and copper together make up just 1 percent of the site inventory. In the earliest chert-rich levels of Nqoma metal objects are rare or nonexistent; in levels contemporary with Divuyu they are more numerous, although still well below quantities dated between AD 900 and 1200, when they double, and, toward the end of this period, triple in abundance. Iron is by far the most abundant metal at both sites at all times; all the identifiable copper objects are items of jewelry, as are 60 percent of iron objects at Divuyu and 75 percent of those at Nqoma. Beads, clips formed around fiber and wood cores, chains, bangles, bracelets, pendants, and rings were fashioned out of both metals, often in combination **(figs. 5.11 & 5.12)**. At Nqoma, a pair of smithing tuyères, along with small quantities of slag knocked off during smithing, and metallurgical evidence for extensive reworking of metal artifacts attest to the creation of much of this jewelry by resident artisans. Tools, mostly barbed arrowheads, needle-like awls, and chisels, are extremely rare. This does not necessarily mean that iron tools were not routinely used, but rather that they were extensively recycled when they broke or wore out. In addition, it could also be that iron was too valuable to squander on tools, which could just as well be made of other materials. While Nqoma was for two, perhaps three, centuries centered on AD 1000 far richer in metal jewelry than any other place in all of southern Africa, all the metal was imported to the site, and this must have

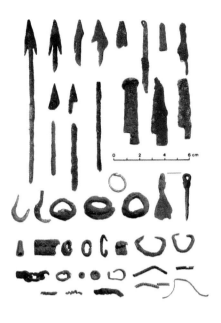

Fig. 5.11 (above):
Divuyu metal.

Fig. 5.12 (above):
Nqoma metal.

entailed costs. One medium for meeting these costs was no doubt the massive quantity of specularite produced from the Hills; indeed, it seems certain that control over specularite mining made it possible for the Nqoma inhabitants to acquire luxury items from a variety of continental as well as Indian Ocean sources.

Wider Connections

The midden at Nqoma is saturated with so much finely pulverized specularite and mica that during excavation everything that came into contact with it became shiny and glistened in the sunlight. The soil matrix also contains massive quantities of angular quartz fragments. This quartz is often the parent rock from which specularite is taken by mining, for which there is considerable evidence in the Hills (fig. 5.13); its presence in such quantity at Nqoma is a sure indication that ore was crushed intensively here before AD 800. In this regard, Nqoma stands in striking contrast to Divuyu, where the few quartz fragments found are probably naturally occurring decay products of the surrounding rocks. Renewed intensity of specularite processing is evident at Nqoma in the seventeenth to eighteenth centuries; this may have been related to stimulants to trade initiated by the Portuguese on the Atlantic Coast of Angola. Glass beads of European manufacture from these centuries and later (fig. 5.14) are scattered in the upper levels of Nqoma, indicating participation in that trade.

Fig. 5.13 (above):
Specularite is often found in quartz.

We can now consider the history of the sites. Stone tool-using, pastoral-foraging people settled on the Nqoma plateau before AD 650, though the evidence necessary to assign a firm date to this occupation is currently inadequate. Almost surely they would have spoken a Khoesan language. Cattle and sheep were kept in small numbers, and wild animals were hunted. They made use of thin-walled pottery, but had no metal. Whether they made their pots or acquired them from others is not clear. The few decorated ceramics do not stylistically resemble early forager-herder wares currently classed as Bambata from sites near Toteng or along the Boteti River, nor can they be

Fig. 5.14
(above):
Nqoma beads.

attributed to currently known Iron Age wares from the region. These early residents of Nqoma were, however, engaged in the processing of specularite in such quantity that a considerable proportion of the finished product must have entered into far-reaching exchange networks. Glass beads of Southeast Asian manufacture and Indo-Pacific marine shells found in these levels suggest that these networks were already connected to the East Coast Indian Ocean trade.

After AD 650, these peoples were joined on the Nqoma plateau by others who made pottery in three distinct styles—some with affinities to Matlapaneng, some with Xaro connections, and some of Divuyu style. These metal-using peoples set themselves up at different locations on the plateau; thin-walled pots were most abundant in the northwest corner of the plateau, where substantial use of stone tools appears to have continued into the second millennium AD. Other households used a variety of other distinctive styles of pottery. Small numbers of sherds from the various styles were distributed in areas other than their principal locations, suggesting that vessels were exchanged among the different households at Nqoma. This, plus the fact that all residents moved on the sand ramp to and from their homes into their wider universe, implies harmonious relations among them. This diversity of ceramic styles and their widely separated geographical sources suggest that this was a multilingual community of both Bantu and Khoesan speakers. Glass beads and marine shells confirm a connection to the East Coast trade; we must assume that specularite was among the commodities exchanged for these luxuries. Livestock were now kept in much greater numbers, with cattle, sheep, and goats each accounting for a third of the faunal remains at Nqoma. At Divuyu, 70 percent of the fauna was goats or sheep; only 5 percent was cattle, probably acquired from Nqoma. The majority of these animals must have been kept elsewhere, as both plateaus are too small to support even token herds. A charred cowpea at Divuyu provides evidence that farming was now part of the economy, but wild plants continued to be gathered.

At about AD 800 (possibly as late as AD 875), the Divuyu plateau was abandoned and never settled again. In addition, Divuyu pottery ceased to be made at the Hills, after a century or more of stylistic stability. At about the same time "classic" Nqoma-style pottery replaced previous styles in all areas of Nqoma. It is not known if the two events were connected, but the replacement was so complete that there can be no doubt that the makers of the newly introduced wares took over the Nqoma plateau. This is the time when the population of Nqoma was most numerous and the artifactual wealth, especially in imported glass beads and marine shells, of its people at its highest. Cattle wealth also increased greatly, and grain agriculture was well established, as confirmed by a mass of charred sorghum seeds on the floor of a house that was destroyed by fire. Significant quantities of quartz were associated with this house, and a pair of smithing bell tuyères was associated with the seed mass (fig. 5.15), as were glass beads and a marine shell along with quantities of metal and ivory jewelry and chert implements. This suggests that an occupant of the house engaged in metal smithing, but not smelting, but also relied on chert for at least some tools. The occupants were also rich in locally produced luxury goods, as well as those derived from long-distance exchange. A contemporary house, also preserved by fire, was similarly endowed with luxury goods. The middens associated with both houses contained large numbers of quartz fragments, confirming that Nqoma peoples were intensely engaged in specularite production at this time.

Fig. 5.15 (above):
Nqoma blacksmith house.

Further evidence for this is provided by a burial dug into earlier levels of the site (fig. 5.16). The soil matrix surrounding this individual, a thirty-five-year-old man, was rich in metal, ivory, and ostrich eggshell jewelry; a glass bead and a cowrie shell were also present. A large quantity of quartz fragments was found in the levels containing the skeleton and two dozen chunks of specularite ore were dispersed in the surrounding matrix; surrounding squares are virtually devoid of this material. This appears to associate the person with mining.

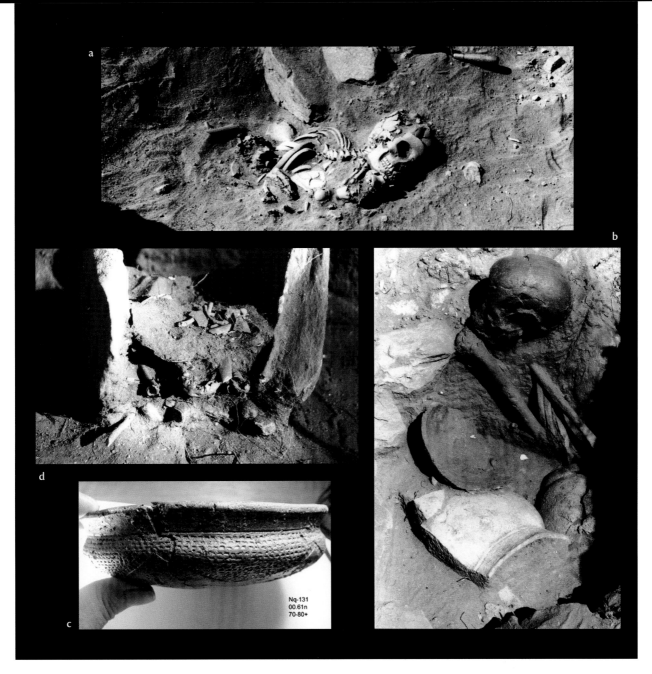

Fig. 5.16 (above):
Nqoma burials (clockwise from top): (a) juvenile burial; (b) adult female burial;
(c) bowl from adult female burial; (d) infant burial.

Conclusion

For about four hundred years, Nqoma was the most distant node in a global trade network extending to the Indo-Asian centers of glass manufacture. The specularite produced by Nqoma people was a significant component of this trade, but evidence from sites such as Toutswemogala in eastern Botswana suggests the inter-regional importance of Tsodilo in this trade began to diminish after about AD 1000, when sources in eastern Botswana began to be extensively exploited. The ocher-slipped bowls of Nqoma type at Bosutswe **(map 0.1)**, for instance, all predate AD 1100. The trans-Kalahari trade in luxury goods, and of intensive specularite production at Tsodilo, came to an end shortly after AD 1200, when K2-Mapungubwe, much nearer to East Coast entrepôts, captured control of the trade. It is clear from the evidence summarized above that stone-using as well as iron-using peoples were engaged in specularite production. Two areas appear to have remained precincts of stone tool users throughout the settlement of the plateau, while others were occupied by a succession of different peoples. This suggests that the multilingual character of current villages in Botswana has a pedigree extending far into the past. ∎

81

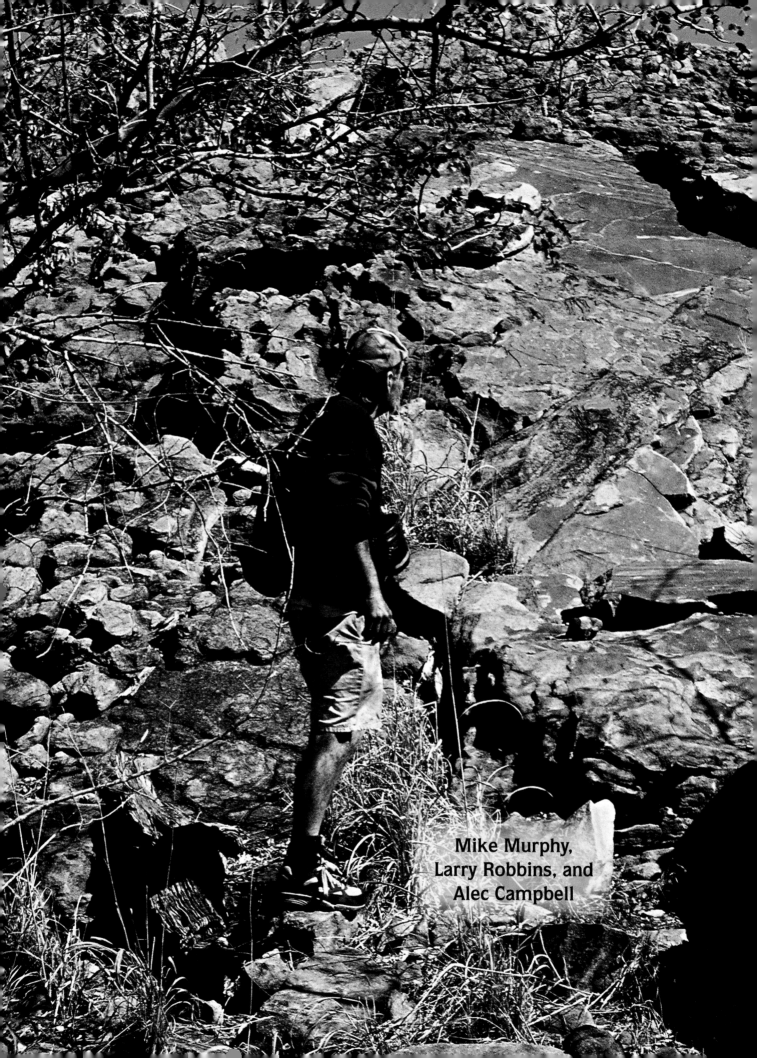

Mike Murphy,
Larry Robbins, and
Alec Campbell

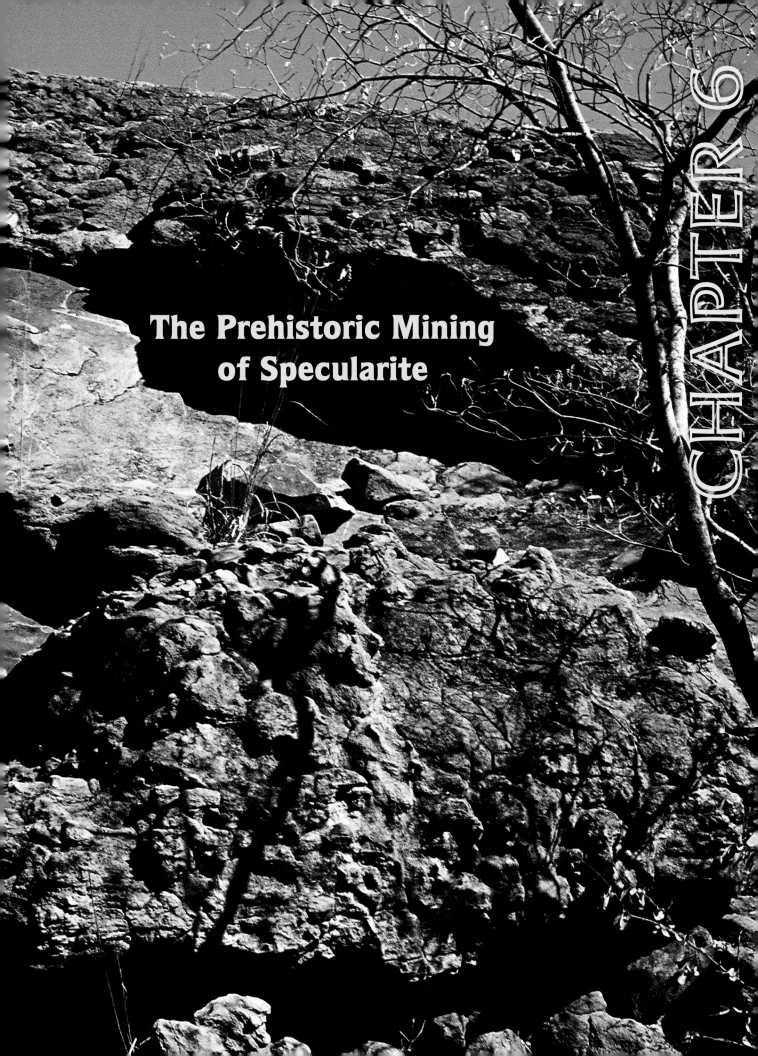

The Prehistoric Mining
of Specularite

Of all the rare and valued resources mined, traded, and owned by prehistoric farmers—from iron, copper, and gold to mica, quartz, chert, and red ocher—none was of more special significance to the peoples of Tsodilo than specular hematite, or specularite.

This was clearly seen in the last chapter in the fact that the midden at the village site of Nqoma contained an abundance of specularite.

Specularite occurs in veins in Tsodilo's bedrock (**fig. 6.2**). It is a highly micaceous hematite, an oxide of iron that sparkles so brilliantly when ground or pulverized that early European travelers, artists, and explorers were moved to describe the glittering black rock. Throughout southern Africa, both Bantu and Khoesan highly valued its cosmetic transformative powers. Yet sources of specularite ore are so extremely rare in the Kalahari that the concentration at Tsodilo must have been of exceptional importance.

What do these mines look like? Who did the mining and when was it done? How did the miners manage to

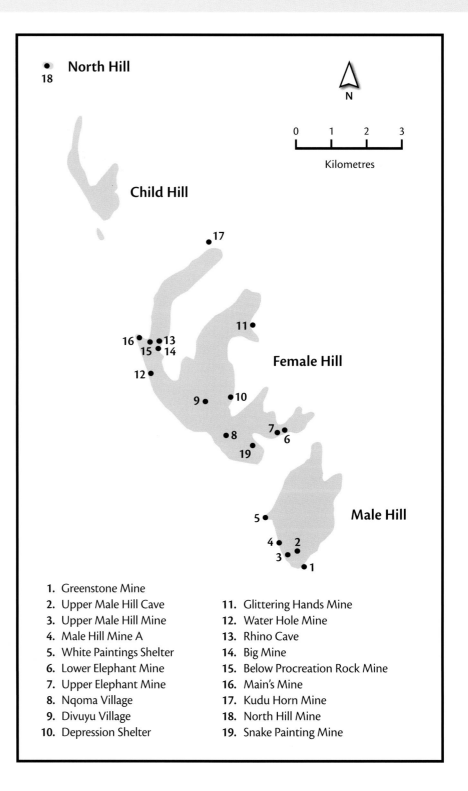

Map 6.1 (right):
Distribution of mines across Tsodilo Hills.

Fig. 6.1 (preceding page):
Open-cast mine above Nqoma. Remains of specularite vein show up as a purple stain on the rock.

1. Greenstone Mine
2. Upper Male Hill Cave
3. Upper Male Hill Mine
4. Male Hill Mine A
5. White Paintings Shelter
6. Lower Elephant Mine
7. Upper Elephant Mine
8. Nqoma Village
9. Divuyu Village
10. Depression Shelter
11. Glittering Hands Mine
12. Water Hole Mine
13. Rhino Cave
14. Big Mine
15. Below Procreation Rock Mine
16. Main's Mine
17. Kudu Horn Mine
18. North Hill Mine
19. Snake Painting Mine

Fig. 6.2 (above):
Veins of specularite in quartzite bedrock.

excavate chambers deep into the hard Tsodilo bedrock, and, finally, why did the complex operations so suddenly come to an end?

The Tsodilo Mines

Mining specularite required an intelligent appreciation of the local geology and good organizational ability. Prospecting is relatively easy once you know which rocks to target; the ore veins are distinctly colored and, where exposed to air and water, produce a particular stain. But once you find them, the grueling work begins. Miners had to know how to follow the veins into the bedrock, how to avoid roof collapses, how to extract the ore from the incredibly hard rock in which it was situated, and lastly how to process it into usable powder.

More than twenty mines have been located at Tsodilo (**map 6.1**). Most mining was done in underground mineshafts and chambers following seams, or veins, of the ore. Excavation of these shafts showed extensive interconnected systems of underground passages, with tailings, or shattered rock debris, either piled at mine entrances or backfilled into areas where the mining was already finished. Most mines follow the horizontal bands of ore seams laterally through the rock, although the entrance shaft of Water Hole Mine angles sharply downward for four meters into bedrock before leveling out and extending another six meters into the hillside. After abandonment, this mine partially filled with water and became known as Tshokgam, the Python Spring.

Some sites are plainly visible; others are remarkably inaccessible and hidden—perhaps intentionally. Most mines resemble shallow caves or fissures, but the deep ones show where miners traced a thick vein in the rock face then chipped into the rock, following the vein both backward and sideways, sometimes extending low passages for ten meters and creating dome-like chambers. Mines vary from about 4.5 to 43 meters long, and 1 to 6 meters wide. Low ceilings, perhaps fewer than 60 centimeters above the floor, can rise in chambers to 2 meters. In back walls veins of specularite appear so thin, less than 20 centimeters wide, that further mining was not worth the effort. In at least one "open-cast" mining area a specularite seam lay so exposed or thinly covered that it was apparently bashed off the bedrock until only a few traces of ore now remain **(fig. 6.1)**.

Rock walls or pillars, left intact to support the roof, suggest the miners did not use pit props and shoring methods. Lacking support technology to extend work deeper, they simply bored in from another angle nearby. Allowing 2.7 grams per hard cubic centimeter and converting the dimensions of mine interiors into volume, we find that in the largest mines people moved a staggering 500 to 1,000 tons of rock. Though it is hard to measure

how much of that rock was specularite, the width of ore veins remaining indicate both the Herculean effort and the precious value of such a miniscule prize.

Big, Greenstone, and Upper Male Hill Mines

Since any original names for these mines have long since faded from memory, we named them on the basis of individual characteristics that impressed us when we discovered them, or in relation to their locations. Three mines stand out. Big Mine, located on Female Hill, has two small entrances about thirty meters apart **(fig. 6.3)**. The lower entrance opens into a sloping chamber ten meters deep; the back is filled with rubble excavated from two parallel, low tunnels which turn out of the left wall of the chamber and, sloping gently upward for some thirty meters, meet just before reaching the upper entrance. In the outer tunnel, a stack of slabs was found at the end of a massive cairn-like rock pile (**fig. 6.4**); on top we found a large hammerstone, perhaps right where it had been left by the last miner. A brown stain covering the walls of the chamber near the lower entrance and reaching almost to its roof indicates that the chamber has filled with water. Below the mine we find crushed rock at what may have been a processing site.

At Greenstone Mine, on Male Hill, the miners excavated seams of ore along the rock face, cutting back to leave a massive shelf some thirty meters long projecting over the excavation. Since mining occurred after or even before it was finished, lengths of the shelf have collapsed, leaving chambers connected now by narrow crawl ways behind the fallen rock. A large internal chamber remains at the southwest end, but, in 2000 a large slab of rock fell from its connecting passage roof, a reminder of how cramped and dangerous mining has always been.

A hard climb brings you to the small but interesting Upper Male Hill Mine (**fig. 6.6**), where specularite occurs in a crystalline form, like lumps of black mica. Initially, ore was chipped from the rock face in two separate places about 30 meters apart. Above the eastern cavity a round tunnel, 1.5 meters in diameter, was "drilled" 4 meters into the rock. Its entry, high on the cliff face, required a ladder or scaffolding. Floor deposit is filled with charcoal, implying the use of fire as a mining tool; one can imagine them lugging firewood over 150 meters straight up the cliff. From what's left of the mine, all that effort extracted not much ore, a sign that crystalline specularite had disproportionate value.

The Findings

Excavating the tailings mounds and inside the mines mostly revealed crude stone tools

Fig. 6.4 (above):
Stack of rock slabs found in outer tunnel of Big Mine.

Fig. 6.3 (left):
Entrance to Big Mine.

Fig. 6.5 (above):
Excavating the tailings pile outside Male Hill Mine A.

and scattered pottery sherds. However, in contrast to the rock shelter excavations, artifacts were generally rare. Protruding from the floor deposit of Male Hill Lower Mine, the few sherds made up a single pot, perhaps used to carry water to pour over hot rocks, cracking them. The long, round, one-to three-kilogram stone hammers came from riverbeds and displayed numerous "bash" marks **(fig. 6.7)**. We found no grindstones or square Iron Age hammerstones, but many large, sharp stone wedges.

The floor in an inner chamber of Greenstone Mine yielded small bladelets and flakes of crystalline quartz; a chert micro-core and flake; hammerstones; incised and undecorated pottery sherds; and small pieces of bedrock, bearing veins of specularite. The bladelets and chert core are typical Later Stone Age artifacts similar to those found at the Tsodilo rock shelters.

How Did They Mine?

After the introduction of iron mining and smelting into southern Africa more than 1,500 years ago, iron tools became available, although these were precious and, as they blunted, were often reworked into smaller and smaller implements. Metal spikes were driven into cracks in the rock with hammerstones, leaving scars still visible on the rock, but Tsodilo mines revealed no scars, no pieces of iron, and no large metal tools for mining or cultivation, all suggesting iron was too valuable a resource for anything but making jewelry or small implements like awls.

Fig. 6.7 (above):
Pick or wedge and hammerstone excavated in Greenstone Mine, Male Hill.

Fig. 6.6 (right):
Upper Male Hill Mine.
Mike Murphy (left) and Larry Robbins stand while the late Alex Matseka is seated. A radiocarbon date obtained on charcoal from the upper hole suggests mining ceased in about AD 950. This is one of the few mines containing crystaline specularite.

Basically, Tsodilo miners appear to have deployed stone hammers, wedges, and fire. With hard rock hammerstones they drove the wedge into a crack with smashing blows, splitting the rock. They pried off thin slabs from the face. They most likely piled knobthorn firewood against a rock face and set it alight to rapidly heat the rock, setting up stresses due to differences in thermal conductivity and expansion between the minerals and the rock surrounding the ore veins. They may well have increased fracturing by pouring water onto the hot expanded rock, causing it to contract and split, after which pieces could be removed with wedges and picks.

Needless to say, this was not delicate work. It would have involved hauling large and small trees long distances and often up the hill, not to mention huge quantities of scarce water carried in skin bags, if water was used at all. They had to remove tons of broken rock from inside the mines and discard it somewhere, near entrances or down the hillside. They had to separate ore from the rock, either at the site or farther away. Since summer days can average 30° C, mining most likely was a seasonal activity conducted during the cooler months of winter.

Dating the Mines

Though people often associate all southern African mining either with Great Zimbabwe (flourishing about AD 1380), or the colonial era, the start of mining at Tsodilo predates those mines by hundreds of years, if not much more. In all, nineteen radiocarbon dates taken from excavated charcoal samples from a dozen mine floors and tailings show a remarkably consistent cluster with no deviations, back to AD 800–1025 (table 6.1). These dates

Table 6.1: Tsodilo Mines Radiocarbon Dates			
Site	**Data B.P.**	**Calibrated (1 sigma)**	**Beta Lab #**
Lower Elephant, tailing, **F**	1,230 ± 60	AD 705–885	84706
Male Hill, A, tailing, **M**	1,210 ± 60	AD 770–890	84715
Lower Elephant, **F**	1,160 ± 60	AD 800–975	84705
Mica Schist (Upper Elephant), **F**	1,150 ± 50	AD 865–975	47863
Main's Mine, **F**	1,140 ± 60	AD 865–985	96237
Greenstone, Lower, **M**	1,120 ± 70	AD 875–1000	96234
Big Mine, alcove, **F**	1,120 ± 60	AD 880–995	84709
Big Mine, centre, **F**	1,110 ± 60	AD 885–1000	84708
Big Mine, upper, **F**	1,100 ± 60	AD 885–1005	84707
Glittering Hands, **F**	1,090 ± 60	AD 890–1010	84710
Male Hill, A, **M**	1,090 ± 60	AD 890–1010	84716
North Hill, **N**	1,080 ± 50	AD 905–920, 950–1010	84718
Kudu Horn, **F**	1,080 ± 50	AD 905–920, 950–1010	84713
Upper Male Hill, **M**	1,080 ± 50	AD 905–920, 950–1010	65194
Greenstone, Lowest, **M**	1,060 ± 60	AD 960–1020	96236
Greenstone, Left, **M**	1,050 ± 60	AD 970–1025	84712
Greenstone, Right, **M**	1,000 ± 50	AD 1000–1040	84711
Greenstone, Lower, **M**	1,000 ± 60	AD 995–1040, 1105–1115	96235
Below Procreation Rock, **F**	960 ± 60	AD 1015–1170	84717

Note: **F** = Female Hill, **M** = Male Hill, **N** = North Hill. Other designations (e.g. A) refer to field names of sites. Dates were processed by Beta Analytic and calibrated following the Pretoria Calibration Procedure program. All dates are from charcoal deposits overlying the floor of mines with the exception of the two tailings dates, which were from charcoal at the base of the tailings.

correlate with the radiocarbon dates available for the settlement at Nqoma, and imply that mining was underway when the settlement was occupied. Yet these dates were taken from the floors of worked-out mines. The time when mining actually started remains unknown. The quartzite bearing specularite seams is an incredibly hard rock and some mines are extensive. Using only fire and stone tools to mine implies that it could have taken thousands of years to excavate mines as big as Greenstone or Big Mine.

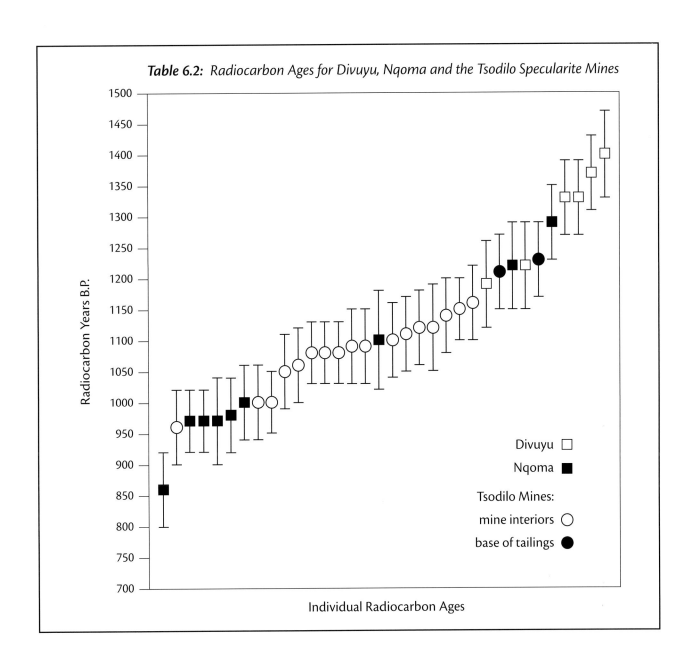

Table 6.2: *Radiocarbon Ages for Divuyu, Nqoma and the Tsodilo Specularite Mines*

Divuyu □
Nqoma ■
Tsodilo Mines:
mine interiors ○
base of tailings ●

Radiocarbon Years B.P.

Individual Radiocarbon Ages

Who Were the Miners?

The earliest miners must have been stone-tool-using people such as those who inhabited Depression and White Paintings Shelters. Surveys in the general area of the mines turned up no miners' villages, nor even smaller miners' work camps.

Several mines have rock paintings at or near their entrances, but most do not. Only one mine has paintings inside it: Snake Mine, a small undated mine that has on its back wall a few small red paintings superimposed by crude white paintings **(fig. 6.8)**. This tells us only that mining here had ceased when the red paintings were made. Test excavation of Upper Cave on Male Hill, close to a mine, produced a few bits of specularite and some Later Stone Age artifacts, but no conclusive signs of occupation by miners.

As discussed in chapter 5, strong links exist between the mines and the settlement at Nqoma. Specularite was clearly being processed at the village of Nqoma, and there was the burial of a man in his thirties who was associated with specularite ore. He was connected to the mines. Yet it is uncertain whether the Nqoma settlers actually mined, although they clearly processed some of the ore and the radiocarbon dates from the mines generally match the

Fig. 6.8 (above):
Back wall of Snake Mine. Two small red paintings, superimposed by white animal images,
indicate that mining here had terminated before painting with red ocher ceased.

dates from Nqoma. However, the crude stone hammers and wedges, the huge quantities of charcoal on mine floors, and the lack of signs of metal tool use certainly suggests mining by Later Stone Age peoples, perhaps continuing an industry they had practiced for thousands of years, and expanding it during Nqoma settlement times, when farmers processed the ore and put it into the trade network that stretched from Tsodilo to the Indian Ocean and beyond.

All this evidence suggests three hypotheses for our possible miners: first, and most probable, stone tool-using foragers who periodically occupied the rock shelters may have exchanged their ore for pottery, iron, and glass beads; second, both stone-using and iron-using peoples collaborated, since the historical record shows different ethnic groups valued specularite; third, iron-using Nqomans organized the mining activities and they processed and traded the ore. These interpretations fit in well with other evidence that Tsodilo was part of a regional economy, where different ethnic groups variously involved with foraging, fishing, and livestock herding all interacted on a regular basis.

Conclusion

It is extremely significant that Tsodilo was mined hundreds or possibly thousands of years before the building of such famous stone-walled sites as Great Zimbabwe; it demonstrates that large-scale labor projects were being carried out in the Kalahari earlier than expected. None of the mines or tailings mounds revealed stratigraphic evidence of distinctive mining episodes separated by periods when the mines were not in use. This finding, consistent with the tight cluster of dates, supports the interpretation that there was a final "burst" of mining activity over a relatively short period.

The fact that three mines, Upper Male Hill, Kudu Horn, and North Hill, located on three different hills yielded identical radiocarbon ages of 1080+/-50 BP (about AD 870) indicates that mining was being carried out at different locations at the same time. Whether these were distinct individual mines competing with each other or were part of one overarching cartel, the work effort would have been substantial.

Food storage capabilities associated with mixed agricultural, herding, and foraging lifestyles would have provided a sufficient food surplus to free a portion of the population to engage in seasonal mining activities. One can envision a larger network of people carrying out the work at several mines at the same time, the Hills literally smoking like a volcano, led by one or several local chiefs.

No one knows exactly what happened to the specularite ore once it had been extracted. Much of it may have been traded with populations throughout the region. Recent chemical analysis of the Tsodilo specularite, when combined with future discoveries of specularite at other sites, will help to define the trade patterns. Adam Kiehn, George Brook, and their colleagues have already learned that the specularite from the Tsodilo mines is different from specularite found at mines located in southeastern Botswana.

Mining at Tsodilo drew to a close at approximately the same time as the end of the earlier occupation at Nqoma; its role in regional and long-distance trade diminished as trade intensified in other areas to the southeast, particularly in the Limpopo Valley. The decline in mining and trade coincides with evidence that the wet climate grew increasingly arid. Specularite mining is fuel-intensive and possibly also water-intensive; two centuries of aggressive processing may have stripped the surrounding landscape of trees and depleted water supplies. Drier conditions may also have inhibited plant growth and water availability, making mining more and more difficult. Perhaps a combination of climatic change, resource depletion, and trade shifts brought an end to mining at Tsodilo. Whatever the case may have been, discovery of numerous ancient mines has added a new chapter, a new layer, to what made Tsodilo Hills so important to so many for so long. ∎

SPECULARITE IN HISTORY

Judging from diaries, specularite was the L'Oreal of the nineteenth-century southern African.

In 1805 Heinrich Lichtenstein wrote of a Tswana woman whose "hair was dressed with great care; it was divided into small bunches, which were well rubbed over with the shining ornament, and hung down from the crown of the head, looking like a profusion of silver thread cords."

William Burchell, in the Northern Cape in 1812, noted "a shining, powdery iron-ore of a steel-grey or bluish lustre," called it by its Tswana name, *sibilo* (sebilo), and believed it was traded over five degrees of latitude. "The mode of preparing and using it, is simply grinding it together with grease and smearing it generally over the body, but chiefly on the head; and the hair is much loaded and clotted with an accumulation of it, that the clots exhibit the appearance of lumps of mineral."

Burchell mixed specularite into his paintings of Batswana wearing the same substance, as in a portrait of Massissan: "Her hair was copiously adorned with *sibilo*; but below the part which has the appearance of a cap, some portion was to be seen of its natural colour and appearance" **(fig 6.9)**.

In 1849, artist-traveler Alfred Dolman described a Molala whose "head was frizzed out with fat and sibilo, literally sparkling like diamonds when he moved. His body was lubricated with red ochre and fat until it acquired a scarlet hue, and carrying a spear 12 feet long on his shoulder." In 1863, Richard Glyn noted at Shoshong: "The girls were draped in all their finery, their heads plastered with tar and grains of mica."

Fig. 6.9 (above): Massissan.

Two other prehistoric specularite mines in southeastern Botswana, Sebilong near Thamaga and Dikgatlampi near Lentsweletau, had both been long abandoned. One still functioning at Blinkklipkop in the Northern Cape was described by John Campbell as "a kind of Mecca to the nations around, who are constantly making pilgrimages to it, to obtain fresh supplies of the blue shining powder and the red stone." At that time, Botswana's Bangwaketse were taking their ivory spoons and sheepskin karosses to Kuruman to trade for, among other items, specularite.

Rock Art
at Tsodilo

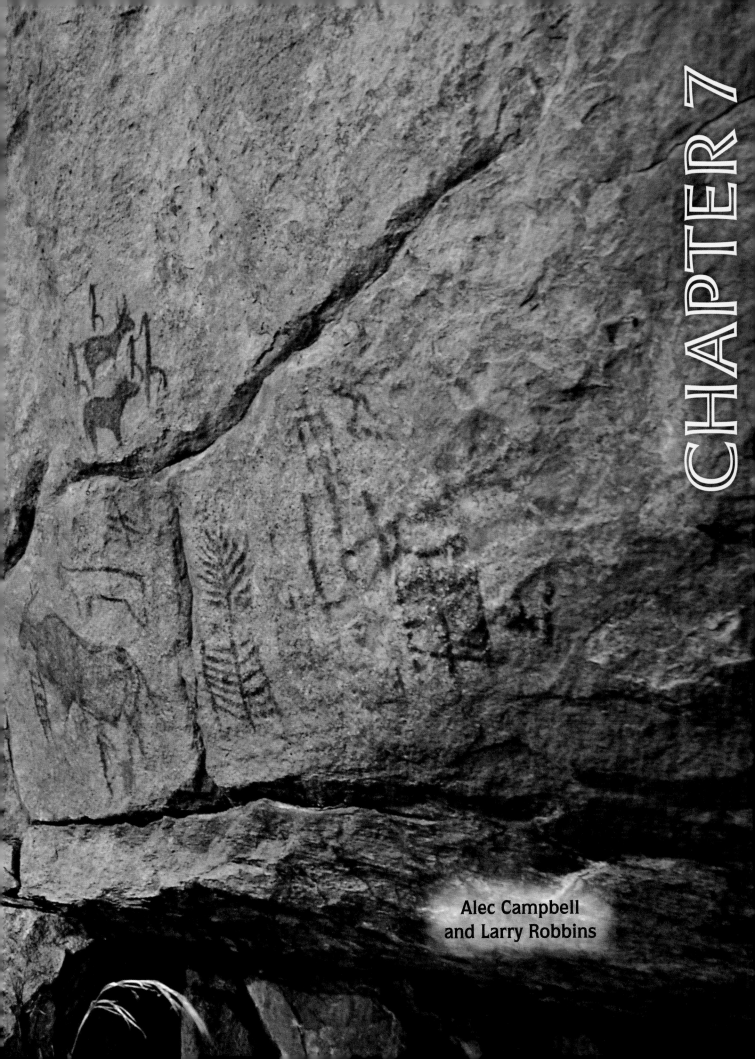

CHAPTER 7

Alec Campbell
and Larry Robbins

M ore than four thousand individual rock paintings depicting animals, people, and geometric designs are scattered at over four hundred different sites across all four Hills.

The art's existence in such an isolated place, deep in the Kalahari Desert, is surprising enough. There are no other rock art sites in the vicinity; the nearest lies in the Gubatshaa Hills, 250 kilometers away on the eastern side of the Okavango Delta (**figs. 7.2 to 7.5**). Since plenty of other rock outcrops in the Kalahari were never painted, there must be something special about this particular stone "canvas" that compelled prehistoric artists to express themselves in pictures on the rock.

Fig. 7.4 (below):
Red shaded painting of domestic bull at Gubatshaa Hills.

Figs. 7.2 (above) & 7.3 (below):
Geometric designs at Gubatshaa Hills differ in style from those at Tsodilo, but bare similarities with some painted designs in Carnarvon District, Northern Cape, South Africa.

Fig. 7.1 (preceding page):
*High on a cliff towards the northwest end of Female Hill, three people, one holding a child by the hand, appear to herd (or steal) two domestic cattle. Below are an eland and predator facing left and a geometric design resembling a plant or fish spine. The upper section of this design is similar to the decoration on a bone excavated in White Paintings Shelter (**fig. 3.8**). To the right are "shield" designs and a red upward-facing ostrich.*

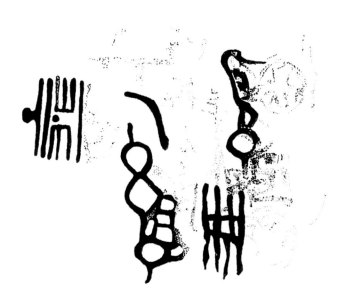

Yet that, too, points to even more surprising differences: the paintings themselves sit uneasily in the general pattern of southern Africa's "San" rock art (known commonly as "Bushman Paintings"); their composition is, in many ways, unique. First, unlike most such paintings, the artists here painted with their fingers, not with brushes. Also, among the images of wild animals, and in similar styles, we find 160 paintings of domestic cattle.

What is more, painted geometric designs appear in a proportion higher here than anywhere else. In contrast to most of southern Africa's human figures, those painted at Tsodilo appear "stick-like" and naked, without bows and arrows, sticks, clothing, or jewelry. Tsodilo's final art episode—crude drawings in white, which are elsewhere generally attributed to black farmers—is here most likely the work of Khoesan peoples. Finally, at Tsodilo we find 2,500 cupules and one hundred grooves hammered and ground into the rock, believed elsewhere to be the oldest surviving symbolic representations made by humans (see chapter 4).

Fig. 7.5 (above):
Red finger paintings on the largest of Gubatshaa's hills. Outline images of eland, elephant, and sable antelope superimpose giraffes. Two zigzag lines back the animals. Although the overlying paintings are similar to Tsodilo images, the decorated giraffe and general composition are different. There are no known zigzag lines at Tsodilo.

The Red Paintings

Finger-drawn art does appear in southern Africa outside of Tsodilo Hills, but never in concentrations like these: some occur in South Africa's Limpopo Province and in the interior of the Western Cape; other somewhat crude "Late White Paintings" are scattered over Central Africa and the southeastern continent. To appreciate this kind of painting, divide their subject matter into three categories: animals, people, and geometric designs.

Animals, mainly large wildlife and cattle, have been drawn in twisted perspective with two horns and two or four legs displayed in silhouette **(fig. 7.17)**. Schematic human figures are often depicted by only two lines, one vertical, bowed and thickened at the middle to denote hips and buttocks, and the other shorter and joined at the thickening to represent a penis. Some display two legs below the thickening and, instead of a penis, have two projections near the top indicating female breasts **(fig. 7.6)**.

Geometric designs include circles and ovals containing grids **(fig. 7.7)** and patterns, "shields" **(fig. 7.8)**, a few handprints, and rows of finger impressions. To these must be added a considerable number of images sometimes described as "stretched skins" **(figs. 7.9 & 7.10)**. Somewhat similar geometric designs have been found in Zambia (mainly painted) and in Angola, Namibia, and northwestern South Africa (usually recorded as engraved). "Stretched skins" (painted) are also found in Malawi and northeastern South Africa.

Fig. 7.7 (above):
*From the Sex site, pass through the neck and descend the path
to bottom of cliff on left. This very faded panel of red circles
containing grids and other designs reflects many individual
paintings found specifically on Female Hill.*

Fig. 7.8 (left):
*Below the Rain-making site and south of Tshokgam, these "shield"
designs occur in a rock alcove. Note the outline eland with
back leg superimposed by a "shield" at bottom left.*

Figs. 7.9 (left) & 7.10 (right): Designs known commonly as "stretched skins". Similar designs occur in neighboring countries. At Tsodilo, these designs usually occur in pairs.

Some sites have paintings of two or more related images—people with cattle, "stick" men and women arranged in lines, and animal groups—though these lack a perspective or background that draws them together into "scenes." Most of Tsodilo's paintings occur haphazardly on the rock face in apparent isolation from each other.

A few Tsodilo artists painted one image either partially or fully over another, a practice called superimposition, common in rock art **(fig. 7.11)** but rare here: red geometric designs may superimpose animals; human figures or images of animals can also superimpose other animals. Yet geometric designs and animals never superimpose human figures, nor do images of cattle ever superimpose other images, all of which may suggest value hierarchies and relationships.

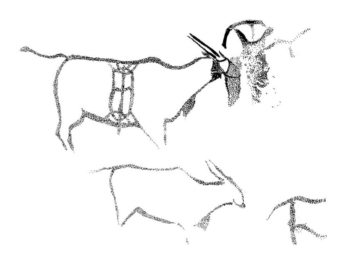

Fig. 7.11 (above):
Red outline eland with geometric design on its body and superimposing its nose.

Fig. 7.12 (above):
Possible ceremony involving a cow, men and women, a person bent at the hips, and a geometric design.

Late White Paintings

Crudely finger-drawn images, made out of a powdery or greasy white paint, and apparently of lime, occur from Kenya to the Eastern Cape and are generally atttributed to Bantu-speakers. For example, in eastern Zambia and Malawi, "white" paintings were made until quite recent times by closed Chewa and Nyau agricultural societies as educational tools for initiates during rites of passage ceremonies.

At Tsodilo, twenty different sites show more than two hundred white paintings, half of them in White Paintings Shelter alone. White paintings include: people with hands on hips facing forward, people riding horses (**fig. 7.13**), a possible wagon wheel and person standing on a wagon, someone dragging a goat, an elephant, a rhino, a giraffe, an eland, cows, antelope, another possible goat, snakes, indeterminate animals, and circular geometric designs including a few "m" shapes.

Although images of people facing the front with hands on hips are found from Tanzania to Botswana (**fig. 7.14**), and "m"-shaped engravings occur in Zambia, the Tsodilo animal drawings are larger and the geometric designs generally less complicated than those found elsewhere. Interestingly, Tsodilo's white paintings not only occur exclusively at sites with earlier paintings in red, but quite often superimpose them, a practice less common anywhere else in Africa.

The Sites

Paintings occur on all four Hills, and by 1994, the official report tallied 20 sites on the small North Hill, 50 on Child Hill, 49 sites on Male Hill, and 266 on Female Hill—an unsurprising endowment for Female Hill, given it is by far the most extensive of the Hills with many peaks, gorges, valleys, and areas of smooth rock. Some 20 more sites have been found since the official count. Most sites occur low down on the western side of the Hills, but some artists sought altitude: one site is situated on an almost inaccessible ledge on Male Hill's cliff face.

A site may have no more than a single isolated painting, a window-sized panel of paintings, a whole wall of paintings, or even clusters of paintings

Fig. 7.13 (above):
*Man riding a horse (see **fig. 3.1** at left end of panel). Horses are believed to have first reached Tsodilo in 1852 with a party of Griqua traders heading for Andara in modern Caprivi.*

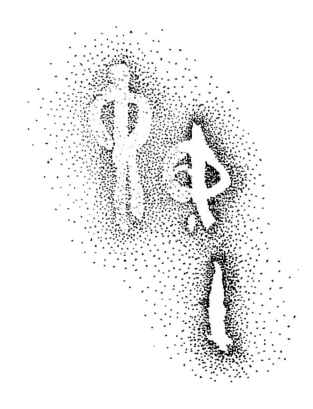

Fig. 7.14 (above):
Men painted in white pigment stand with hands on hips. Child Hill.

Fig. 7.15 & 7.16 (above):

A few hundred meters north of Rhino Trail, a panel of white geometric designs is brightened by the evening sun. Note in the tracing how a white oval and circle in the middle of the panel superimpose a red geometric design. The white paintings are recent, perhaps drawn by Ncaekhwe who for several centuries were recognized as the "owners" of Tsodilo.

stretching for twenty or more meters along a cliff face. Perhaps 0.05 percent of the painted sites were ever inhabited —Rhino Cave, an open site on Child Hill, Depression, White Paintings, and Dancing Penises shelters—again in marked contrast to those throughout southern Africa, which experts believe most likely were occupied. Nor is the ground in front of most sites suitable for living, dancing, or ceremonies involving numbers of people. Instead paintings occur on exposed rock and cliff faces or have broken rocky ground below them. Although most painted sites face to the west, this is governed more by geological disposition than by human intention; that is, for reasons intrinsic to the Hills themselves, rather than for conduciveness to either residence or performance of ceremonies.

Paint and Painting Methods

People derived paint from crushed, and possibly burned, stones mixed with a liquid binder. For colors they used stones containing oxidized iron to make shades of red and orange; limonite for yellow; gypsum and lime or calcrete for white; and manganese oxide, specularite, or charcoal for black. They mixed colored pigments to get different shades; red darkened with specularite made purple. Excavations at Depression and White Paintings Shelters revealed bits of red and black hematite, white calcrete, and smooth, plate-sized stones stained with red that may have been used as palettes.

It is harder to determine the various adhesives, or "binders." Suggestions have included blood, egg whites, urine, animal fat, plant juice, honey, snake venom, eagle droppings, water, and even semen. A Ncae man living west of Tsodilo, who said he was descended from the painters, claimed that powdered pigment from the Xeidum Valley was mixed in a duiker's skin with fat from around a cow's heart. We found the pigment deposit, an ancient bed of rotted cyperus reeds. Underground it was black, but when exposed to light it turned red. People who live near the deposit still use the red pigment to paint images on the exterior walls of their houses, such as a large giraffe that adorned one wall.

In Lesotho in 1930, Mapote, a man with half-San brothers, told the anthropologist Marion How that eland's blood was used to mix red; plant juices to mix white; burnt stick charcoal and water to mix black. When Mapote painted an eland, for demonstration, he made a number of brushes by inserting quills of tiny feathers into the ends of reeds, and used a different brush to apply each color to the rock. Tsodilo's artists may have mixed crushed pigment with a binder, carried it in small antelope horn containers, liquefied it at the site, and then drawn with their fingers across the rock face.

Tsodilo paintings have none of the fine lines found in most San rock art; they appear to have been drawn rather than painted. With a few exceptions, they are red, or two shades of red. Most have a thick outline, perhaps drawn with the finger, then in-filled by a lighter shade of the same color, applied with the palm. The art that remains is often faded or indistinct, suggesting that many earlier paintings may have lost their original freshness, lost their color, or vanished entirely (**fig. 7.17**). It is wrenching to imagine what masterpieces may have been lost to the ravages of time. On the other hand, at sites like the Dancing Penises Shelter, paintings have either been touched up or strengthened at a time after their original painting (**fig. 7.26**).

Fig. 7.17 (left):
In Gubekho Gorge on the right slope and beyond the spring, an eland with calf. The animals were first painted with the fingers in outline and then the bodies filled in. One back and one front leg, and the head painted in twisted perspective with two ears and horns visible. Much of the antelope painting at the left of the panel has disappeared, either through erosion or fading.

Dating the Paintings

Because the existing paintings primarily occur on rock faces exposed to sun, rain, and wind, it is doubtful if any of them are very old. Even paintings of cattle are often badly faded, although that animal did not appear near Tsodilo until some two thousand years ago.

Scientifically dating rock paintings has proved exceptionally difficult because little or no suitable organic pigment to date remains on the rock. Scientists are experimenting with accelerator mass spectrometry (AMS) dating, which requires only a tiny amount of blood or plant sap used to bind the pigment. The AMS technique has been used successfully to date European cave art where charcoal was sometimes used in the pigment.

There is a regional context for a range, however, which indicates rock art in southern Africa has ancient roots. The oldest come from Blombos Cave, where two pieces of ocher engraved with diamond patterning have been dated to over seventy-seven thousand years ago. These engravings are symbolic expressions and an early step toward art. Apollo 11 Cave in Namibia yielded another date, between eighteen thousand and twenty-seven thousand years ago, on archaeological deposits containing seven small portable stones bearing painted animals.

Cattle paintings may help to date Tsodilo art. The same styles and colors used—outline, outline in-filled, and one back and front leg with head drawn in twisted perspective—suggest that cattle and wild animals were drawn by the same artists during the same time periods. So most art was probably drawn during the first millennium AD, when cattle were of great importance at Tsodilo.

Likewise, the first horses known to reach Tsodilo belonged to a party of Griqua traders who passed near the Hills on their way to Andara in 1852, the earliest probable date for the drawings of men mounted on horses **(fig. 7.13)**. The late Gcau, a Juc'hoansi, once said his grandfather, who would have been alive in 1880, had drawn some of the white paintings. He later denied this, but other Juc'hoansi confirmed that Gcau's grandfather did draw at least one image using ash of *motswere* (*Combretum imberbe*). Hambukushu admit they used the paintings in White Paintings Shelter, but deny authorship, saying they found the paintings there on their arrival in the 1860s.

Fig. 7.18 (above):

High on a cliff on Female Hill, red outline drawing of a cow superimposed by two geometric designs. These images, in the same style as those depicting wild animals, clearly indicate that cattle form an integral element of Tsodilo's art, dating at the same time as many of the animal paintings.

We do not know when red painting ceased, but this could have occurred in the twelfth century, when Tsodilo ceased to be a major trade center and apparently the cattle population collapsed. Painting in white may have started after the collapse. Since white paintings superimpose red, but never the reverse, we can assume they are later than red art.

Thus it is possible to determine a rough chronology for Tsodilo's paintings, using fading as another criterion. The earliest art appears to be silhouette images of larger animals such as rhino, antelope, and giraffe, drawn in in-filled outline, usually with only one leg back and front, accompanied by faded round geometric designs. The second period may be represented by human figures, outline animals, brighter round designs, square designs, and finger marks. The final period includes paintings in white.

Who Were the Artists?

Tsodilo's red finger paintings fit comfortably neither into fine-line San brush paintings nor into cruder late art done in white by farming peoples. Indeed Tsodilo's paintings more closely resemble rock engravings on southern Africa's inland plateau than they do San paintings. Consider their haphazard placement on open rock faces, the large numbers of geometric designs, the smaller proportion of human to animal images, and the outline and silhouette styles. So who created them?

It seems possible that the red paintings, which include at least 120 identified images of cattle and possibly an additional 40 faded images that appear to be cattle, were painted by peoples who either herded or were closely involved with cattle. Another possibility is that the original settlers of Nqoma made these paintings. As discussed in chapter 5, they were almost certainly Khoesan peoples, who made stone tools and herded livestock. In addition, they occupied Tsodilo at the probable time when most of the red paintings were made.

According to both Juc'hoansi and Hambukushu the paintings were made by God. Three Juc'hoansi men—Gcau, Shoroka, and Xauwe—took us to a panel of painting on Child Hill that included geometric designs of "ladders," an ostrich, and an eland **(figs. 7.19 & 7.20)**. They said that when their ancestors arrived here in the 1860s, the Ncaekhoe then living there told them that this panel was still "alive" and worked for them. They agreed that Ncae ancestors had been involved with the paintings and eventually said that Ncae may have held the pigment, but God had guided their hands to create the images. A Ncae man in the Xeidum Valley west of Tsodilo said his ancestors had made the paintings but was either unable or reluctant to ascribe meanings to the images.

The Ncaekhoe are a Central San people speaking a language related to the Naro and Gcwi languages of Ghanzi and to Nama of Namibia. Nama and Naro both employ their own words for domestic animals and Nama people are known to have a history of pastoralism. Juc'hoansi, the current San occupants of Tsodilo, on the other hand, are a Northern San people, speak a language unrelated to Central San, and use borrowed words for domestic animals. It is possible that some or many of the cattle images mentioned above were painted by pastoral ancestors of Ncaekhoe.

The authors of the white paintings are also difficult to determine. It is unlikely that the white paintings could have been made by Hambukushu. Samutjau, worrying that his people's history might be lost, has during recent years described some of their cultural traditions that are not usually shared with others. It would appear unlikely that he would firmly deny authorship to his ancestors if they had, in fact, been the artists. He said the paintings depicting men on horseback may have been made by the horsemen themselves. While much cruder, the white paintings reflect the red ones: they include large wild animals such as elephant, rhino, giraffe, and antelope; they include cattle and circles containing grid forms. All this could suggest they are merely a later occurrence of the red tradition, drawn by peoples with beliefs and lifestyles similar to those of the earlier artists. They may also be the work of more recent Ncae immigrants.

The pivotal question remains: to whom did the cattle in the paintings belong? Were they the property of the artists, the farmers, or both? Cattle bones were found in the farming village middens but never in any rock shelter. If pastoral Khoe, other than possibly the earlier inhabitants of Nqoma, ever lived at or near Tsodilo, their village sites have not yet been found. The cattle may have belonged to pastoral Khoe who performed their own rituals for their cattle. Future research may answer this question.

Figs. 7.19 (left) & 7.20 (above):
The site on Child Hill that Gcau, Shoroka, and Xauwe said the Ncaekhoe had told their ancestors still worked for them in about 1850. Note the "shield" designs; there are no red circular designs on either Male or Child Hills.

Interpreting Tsodilo's Rock Art

Images are symbols; they may reflect a hidden meaning or identity. A painting of an eland could symbolize health or plenty rather than the animal itself. Over time, the paintings carried different meanings to different people who painted and used them for different purposes.

In an age of airplanes, diesel borehole pumps, antibiotics, and automobiles, the Juc'hoansi and Hambukushu resident here still consider the Hills to be alive and treat them with deep respect. How much more did ancient peoples fear their power and find means to appease their Spirits? The paintings almost certainly have spiritual significance that may well be related to the Hills on which they occur.

With few obvious scenes involving people, it's hard to interpret the earlier animal images drawn in isolation from each other, albeit sometimes on the same rock. Apart from their species, nothing gives them meaning. Giraffe, eland, and rhino are by far the most common, followed by elephant, gemsbok, and cattle. Modern San consider these important sources of meat, and recognize the former three as involved with rainmaking; some of their bones were excavated in Tsodilo's shelters (table 7.1).

Most of the animals listed opposite that were found at White Paintings Shelter were excavated in Later Stone Age deposits. All of the identified bones were from wild animals, with the exception of a single sheep jaw that was contemporaneous with the Tsodilo village site of Divuyu, where domestic animals were common. Reedbuck, lechwe (an antelope), Angoni vlei rat, bushbuck, bushpig, cormorant, ducks and geese, and fish indicate nearby water and wetland. Klipspringer, a small antelope adapted to rocky outcrops, does not occur at Tsodilo but they are found in Namibia. Cape zebra and giant hartebeest are extinct animals that lived during the Pleistocene, or Ice Age, at least ten thousand years ago.

Animal bones were not common at other Tsodilo rock shelter excavations, possibly due to poor preservation conditions as well as other factors. Depression Shelter yielded hare, springhare, warthog, steenbok, gray duiker, bird, snake, and tortoise. Rhino Cave produced unidentifiable bone fragments and tortoise, while some small bone fragments and the jaw of a steenbok were found at Ancestors' Cave. Notice that the rock paintings contain many animals not found in the shelter excavations and vice versa. However, the animals from the shelter cover a considerable time span within the Later Stone Age. Nonetheless, it can be seen that a great range of animals were known to the people of Tsodilo, who also painted human figures. Many of the above animals still occur at Tsodilo, or were found at Tsodilo during the recent past.

Images of people are invariably stick-like, distinguished either by penis or breasts. Some scenes have both figures, which may merely denote gender rather than sexual virility and fertility.

When cattle first appeared in the art, they may have been crucial to the local economy, at the same time human figures began to occur. Those rare scenes involve people with cattle, or men with erect penises, sometimes accompanied by women with breasts. In one well-painted scene three adults, one leading a child, appear to be either herding or stealing cattle (fig. 7.1). At three other sites, cattle are associated with what may be mythical rain animals, and at one of these a rain animal squirts four streams from its udder area into a geometric design (figs. 1.11 & 1.12). The number of similar scenes involving people and cattle suggests a ritual activity, while those of cattle and rain animals may involve rainmaking.

Red geometric designs pose a different problem. Found singly or grouped, sometimes occurring with animals and sometimes with people, they conform to specific patterns and must have symbolic meaning. Ben Smith, using modern Pygmy designs made on bark-cloth by women, and general African beliefs, argues that Zambia's geometric designs represent weather and fertility symbols, made by women, while animal depictions were the work of men. Because of the "trail" of geometric art down the western subcontinent, and because of general similarities of design along its route, Tsodilo's geometric art may fit into Smith's hypothesis. Thus, women may have painted geometric designs related to weather control and human fertility.

Table 7.1: *Comparison of Animals Identified in Excavation at White Paintings Shelter and Animals Identified in Rock Paintings*

White Paintings Shelter	Tsodilo Rock Paintings	White Paintings Shelter	Tsodilo Rock Paintings
Lesser red musk shrew *		Blue wildebeest	Blue wildebeest
Hare	Hare	Impala	
Springhare		Gray duiker	
Damaraland molerat		Klipspringer	
Pouched mouse		Steenbok	Steenbok
Hairy-footed gerbil		Sheep	
Bushveld gerbil *		Buffalo **	Buffalo (?)
Angoni vlei rat		White-breasted cormorant	
Porcupine		Helmeted guineafowl	
Vervet monkey		Francolin	
Bat-eared fox		Ducks / geese **	
Honey badger		Ostrich (eggshell)	Ostrich
Genet		Hingeback tortoise	
Mongoose **		Leopard tortoise	
Hyena **	Hyena	Monitor lizard	
Wildcat		African python	Python
Caracal *		Catfish **	
Leopard	Leopard	Cichlids (tilapia) **	Fish / whale
Aardvark (antbear)	Aardvark (antbear)		Kori bustard
Plains zebra	Zebra		Gemsbok
Cape zebra			Baboon (?)
White rhinoceros	Rhinoceros		Cow
Elephant	Elephant		Goat
Warthog	Warthog		Horse
Bushpig			Sable antelope
Giraffe	Giraffe		Hippopotamus
Eland	Eland		Jackal
Greater kudu	Kudu		Lion
Bushbuck			Cheetah
Roan antelope *	Roan antelope		Wild dog
Lechwe *			Scorpion (?)
Southern reedbuck *			Crab (?)
Hartebeest and/or Tsessebe	Hartebeest / Tsessebe		Mythical animal
Giant hartebeest			Mythical snake

* Probable identification	Excavated animals were identified by
** Animal identified but species indeterminate	R. Klein, R. Milo, N. J. Stevens, J. A. Holman,
(?) Uncertain identification	K. M. Stewart (fish), and G. Avery (birds).

By contrast, square geometric designs, also known as "shields," may incorporate three vertical lines that extend like arms, legs, and a head, three above and two below a square "body." They range from simple configurations to intricate pictographs possibly representing human forms. At the extreme, they become similar to the images of "stretched skin." Some may have penises and testicles, which suggest the square designs represent males, and circle designs, females.

Circular designs may superimpose an animal's nose or hip, never the whole animal. Square geometric designs may be placed within an animal's outline, but never over the outline itself. Superimposition may be the enhancement of the symbolic meaning of the animal superimposed.

David Lewis-Williams proposes that geometric designs are records of entoptic phenomena—patterns floating before the eyes of shamans entering the trance state. Perhaps, but Tsodilo's geometric designs—here painted, elsewhere engraved—fit without much difficulty into the broad trail of geometric art that stretches from southern Congo down Africa's drier western inland plateau to the Orange River. This broad trail itself suggests continuity over a huge distance spreading from regions where Twa, autochthonous gatherer-hunters, lived into areas of ancestral San art. In southern Africa, engraved geometric designs (and the painted designs of Tsodilo) are thought to be relatively recent, made during the last 1,500 years.

Using Rock Art at Tsodilo

The Juc'hoansi easily recognize the different animal species depicted, with the interesting exception of cattle. They claim (wrongly) the only cattle painting is the one in black at Rhino Panel (**figs. 7.21 & 1.5**), which Europeans told them was painted by ancestral Bantu-speakers. The reason for this exclusion is uncertain, but may be because they want the paintings to be purely "San" and have been told by others that San never owned cattle.

Fig. 7.21 (above):
Drawing in black outline of a cow on Rhino Panel
(**fig. 1.5**), *the only image at Tsodilo that*
older Juc'hoansi claimed to be a cow.

According to Samutjau Mukate, the headman at Tsodilo, Hambukushu believe that white pigment reflects masculinity, purity, and calm; red is feminine and dangerous. White geometric paintings are involved with the forehead, "*phatlha*," and provide a direct route through a "window" to the object of desire (in Setswana, the action of *lebagana*, or facing directly forward from the forehead). To him, the geometric paintings are symbols more than tools. Yet paintings clearly helped people proceed directly to things sought or to see into another dimension, to locate particular game species, to find lost cattle, to access the ancestors who live inside the rocks.

Because red geometric designs were seen as extremely dangerous, white paint drawn over the individual lines of a red design changed its aspect, softening and calming it. Samutjau said his ancestors used red animal paintings as a form of immobilizer (he used the Tswana word *kgato*), and described how a burning coal was put below such an image by hunters wishing to prevent game from moving away. When the animal was killed, its liver was placed below the painting.

Although Hambukushu have no known history of painting on rocks at Tsodilo, they once performed trance dances that use paintings and a site. Indeed, while Samutjau denied his ancestors painted images, he maintained they had used one of the paintings in White Paintings Shelter, which had special significance. He described how ancestor spirits, *mandengura*, might possess people, make them wander up into the Hills, and must be controlled in a special healing ceremony.

His ancestors would visit White Paintings Shelter and beat drums to bring the possessed person down from the Hills. Three special drummers stood below the drip-line (the edge of the shelter's natural overhang) facing out of the shelter, each with a long drum tied between his knees, one base and two trebles. The shelter acted as a resonator, causing the sound of drumming to travel over a great distance. While drummers played, people danced, singing a song to the Hills, clapping in time, picking up the chorus between verses.

As the rhythm mesmerized, dancers might enter a trance state and, as people sang, face the shelter wall, pointing to a white circle design to attract the spirit within the Hills. The possessed person at first remained inanimate, but later was, of his or her own accord, drawn into the dancing and singing. Once the possessed danced and sang in time with the others, he or she was cured. Samutjau's wife sang the song for us, gently clapping her hands in time:

A we diwe	You, Hill
Shira wa pira murongo o yo	Living without any river
Ku kara ze morahura	Your water dries up in the sand
Shira wa pira murongo	Living without a river
Chorus: *Shira wa pira murongo.*	

Southern African Rock Art

Rock art in southern Africa may be divided into paintings mostly drawn with a brush rather than painted, and engravings pecked or scraped into exposed rock using a pointed stone.

Paintings may again be divided into earlier paintings, with red the dominant color, and more recent white paintings, although, since about AD 500 the two forms overlap. Red paintings are generally attributed to ancestors of San, while white paintings are mostly the work of Bantu-speaking farmers. There are no clear divisions in the engravings, although they probably have the same time frame as the paintings.

Throughout southern Africa similarities pervade the red, or what are generally described as San ("Bushman"), paintings: wild animals, human figures, and designs. From area to area, images vary in form. Perspective is sometimes difficult to comprehend as "scenes" lack environmental backgrounds. Painted images often employ thin lines, tiny dots, and details that could only have been made with a brush or spatula. Thus, San painting is often known also as "fine-line" painting.

On southern Africa's inland plateau, particularly in drier regions, the art no longer fits snugly into the general fine-line pattern. Fine-line painting tends to be replaced in many areas by engravings, although generally depicting similar motifs. However, numerical proportions differ: human figures dominate "fine-line" art, followed by animals, while earlier geometric designs are rare. Among engravings, animal and geometric designs far outnumber human figures. Where the inland art is painted, images were drawn with fingers rather than painted with brushes.

More recent engravings and most inland finger paintings are attributed to herders, click-speakers who may have entered southern Africa through Botswana some two thousand years ago.

Red fine-line paintings and earlier engravings were made by ancestors of San hunter-gatherers, peoples who have a long history of residence in the southern continent.

Although differences in painting and engraving styles occur across southern Africa, much of the art tends to reflect a hunter-gatherer lifestyle and expresses similar concepts of the natural world and human participation in it: what may be described as a single worldview. Tsodilo's art fits, although somewhat clumsily, into this general worldview.

Another Comparison: The Western Rock Art Trail

A feature of the art that stretches from western Uganda and southern Democratic Republic of Congo is a widespread trail of geometric designs. In the north, these designs tend to take the form of circles, concentric circles, spirals, and circles with external spikes, usually painted in red with a faded white in-fill, but sometimes also engraved. In Zambia, painted "ladders," lines, and finger-marks are added. Moving south through Namibia to the Northern Cape and across southern Africa's inland plateau, similar, although usually engraved, geometric designs continue in abundance. The trail ends more or less on the Orange River.

The Tsodilo Hills are situated at the middle of this broad trail, and much of the Hills' art fits fairly snugly into the trail's general art pattern. In addition, there are a group of rock paintings in the isolated Gubatshaa Hills two hundred and fifty kilometers to the east of Tsodilo **(figs. 7.2, 7.4 & 7.5)**. Sixty-three finger paintings of animals, including one of a cow, and geometric designs, but no people nearly reflect Tsodilo's art. Tsodilo and Gubatshaa provide the trail with a broad stepping-stone across a long stretch apparently otherwise devoid of painted rock art sites.

Interpreting "San Paintings"

Originally, rock art recorders thought that San painting was "art for art's sake" and that it recorded actual events, visually expressed folklore, or was used as sympathetic magic for success in hunting. However, much rethinking has been occasioned by a number of factors. These include concentration on a limited variety of animal species, such as the eland in South Africa and the female kudu in Zimbabwe, and the almost total exclusion from the art of a wide variety of other species.

Over the last thirty years, many researchers, led by David Lewis-Williams, have concluded that "San paintings" reflect shamanism and were made by healers, mainly men but also women, able to enter a trance state during dance to contact and utilize supernatural powers for human benefit. The paintings, they believe, depict the visions and experiences the shamans saw during their trance states and thus were religious expressions. Nor were they just religious expressions, but "reservoirs of potency and mental imagery" that strengthened and molded the community. The paintings were, in fact, artifacts and could have been used in their own right for purposes such as healing, reaffirming community cohesion, and rainmaking.

Other researchers, while accepting that shamanism was the art's central motif, see many of the more mundane images of animals and humans, such as those lacking a mystical nature (humans with animal heads, flying buck, mythical animals, ritual activities, and so on), as secular rather than religious. Some have suggested that the images reflect folklore and myth rather than religious experience, but a difficulty here lies in the animals and humans depicted. San myths tend to emphasize birds, reptiles, and women, while the actual art concentrates more on eland, antelope, giraffe, smaller mammals, and people, usually men.

One thing is really important. When trying to understand rock art symbolism, including Tsodilo's paintings, one must put aside the immediate interpretations one makes based on the shape of images. A prehistoric forager painting an eland must have known he or she was painting an eland. Yet an eland for him or her, as it still does for San today, may have symbolized fat, plenty, health, rain, water, and the animal's magical power to assist in difficult rites of passage when boys and girls enter adulthood. People with animal heads could have represented shamans in trance imbued with the power of the animals whose head they bore. Large animal images resembling a cross between bulls and hippopotami are found in many regions of southern Africa and are similar to mythical rain animals seen in trance and described by modern San shamans.

Rock Art Walking Trails at Tsodilo

The National Museum has established and cleared three rock art trails; a guide should accompany those venturing beyond them. Yet visitors do not have to follow the trails in any order, pace, or sequence. You'll find six sites ranged along the base of the cliff in front of the Site Museum, five sites at White Paintings Shelter, and four sites close to Rhino Panel. There are three other unmarked trails.

Rhino Trail offers the best variety of rock art and can be walked comfortably in either direction in four hours. Its highlights include: numerous red animal and geometric paintings, some white animal and geometric paintings, a very few handprints, a few human depictions, one outline image in black of a cow, two cupule sites, and the place where God lowered cattle onto the Hills when the rocks were still soft. Gubekho Gorge **(fig. 7.24)**, at the start of the trail, is a steep, short climb; older people sometimes prefer to walk the trail in reverse and descend Gubekho Gorge at the end of the walk rather than climb it at the start of the trail.

Fig. 7.22 (left): A rare scene: an antelope, possibly a tsessebe, appears to feed while a second antelope leaps up, apparently startled.

Fig. 7.23 (left): Paintings of antelope, rhino, and giraffe above a ledge and next to the path up the initial climb into Gubekho Gorge.

Lion Trail takes about two-and-a-half to three hours to walk, includes a short distance along Rhino Trail, and involves no climbing. Sites include a few animal paintings, Rhino Panel, Dancing Penises Shelter, Lion Site, White Paintings Shelter, two cupule sites, and a prehistoric mine.

Cliff Trail commences at the campsite below Tshokgam, the Python Spring (**fig. 1.10**) and follows the base of the cliff northward, climbs over a pass into a central valley and then turns westward up the sloping rocks, passes over the top of the cliff, and descends by a difficult route to the cliff base. It takes at least four hours, passes numerous paintings sites, the place where sex was created, a number of prehistoric mines, and white geometric designs. Use a guide.

Divuyu Trail commences in the large central valley of Female Hill, climbs up and passes over the Hill, and takes about four or five hours. It holds few rock art sites but offers spectacular views and a wide variety of vegetation. This trail requires a guide.

Northern Trail circles the north end of Female Hill and passes several prehistoric mines, the Crab, Stolen Cattle, Museum Zebra, and Sex sites, two groove sites, and an area where pigment may have been burnt for paintings. The trail takes four to five hours. For all trails, carry a bottle of water and some food, wear sensible shoes or boots and a hat, and keep arms and legs covered. ■

Fig. 7.24 (above):
The steep climb into Gubekho Gorge. The paintings in **fig. 7.23** *are situated above a ledge on the right side of the path and the paintings in* **fig. 7.22** *are situated at the top of a steep climb leading off the path just before the spring is reached.*

Fig. 7.25 (right):
Close to the start of Divuyu Trail and on the left of the path, this painting of a hippopotamus and dancing person superimposes a very faded giraffe.

The last six chapters have explored a significant part of the Tsodilo Hills story, leading us from the environmental changes of the past through the archaeological sites and the rock paintings. None of this work would have been possible without the assistance of the staff of the National Museum of Botswana over many seasons. For this reason, it is appropriate at this point to include a personal account about this work before moving into present-day issues.

Fig. 7.26 (right):
Dancing Penises Shelter lies about three hundred meters from Rhino Panel and on Lion Trail. Men marked by penises and women with breasts appear to perform a ceremony involving a domestic cow (top left).

From 1995 through 2005 I had the extraordinary opportunity to dig and sift alongside Larry Robbins, Alec Campbell, Mike Murphy, Leonard Ramatokwane, George Brook, and Shaw Chen. Not all of us at once, of course, but I was always a full member of their team. Our team began working at the Rhino Cave and excavated some very fascinating Stone Age deposits. Yet as with so many things in life, it was the process as much as the product, the camaraderie as much as the conclusions, that we most remember and value.

I recall once, while excavating, how a large boulder appeared in one of the squares; this obstacle hampered our work and led to many frustrations. But eventually, after working together to extend the trench a further two meters, we managed to continue. Before time ran out we discovered Later Stone Age artifacts and some Middle Stone Age deposits in the cave floor. That left enough enticement to bring us back the following year to conduct further excavations.

I found the excavation work enthralling. It didn't seem so much like "work" when you were collaborating with energetic colleagues who were so eager to share what they had with others. It was more like a serious, adult form of disciplined "play."

Of course the glamour can wear thin. During the excavation, I did a lot of sieving and sorting. At first, I did not like either activity, but as time went on, I began to take pleasure in sieving because, with a more experienced eye, that's where the most interesting artifacts emerged. Even sorting grew more enjoyable as I learned to distinguish different kinds of artifacts, combined with their archaeological significance. Upon discovering specularite crystals, for example, we could demonstrate that there were mines nearby.

I also had the opportunity of descending the seven-meter hole at the White Paintings Shelter **(fig. 7.27)**. Deep, dark holes like that can bring out the claustrophobe in anyone; while folded down inside the hole a thought would occur to me like, "Say, what if the walls collapsed?"

"Well, then I would be buried alive and that's all there is to it."

During such silent conversations with myself, I felt the fast heartbeat of adventure. I also felt the cold sweat of fear. But by pushing myself deeper, I sought to venture further into the archaeology of the area. Our curiousity to know what lay beneath was rather "spoilt" by the decision to stop digging because of the danger of wall collapse. My lingering curiosity remains matched only by my relief.

Fig. 7.27 (above):
Entrance to the seven-meter excavation
made at White Paintings Shelter.

Rock paintings, by contrast, are so fragile that they require constant and delicate concentration. One should not touch them with bare hands, I discovered, because doing so might leave permanent marks. Recording rock art paintings can prove tedious and slow but, once again, I began to realize the importance of the work and found interest in the challenge of preserving what is merely ephemeral into something eternal.

I especially liked the geometric paintings, which are painted with white pigment (**figs. 7.28 & 7.29**). These are believed to be recent as compared to those dominant red ocher paintings. Most paintings were neatly painted and, because they represented human figures or animals, more easily recognized. We soon appreciated the invaluable help of local people in identifying some of the "invisible" paintings that a lifetime of residence has made plain to them. Tsodilo's residents also provided us with oral histories of some places in Tsodilo and stories of people who may relate to a particular area.

We also recorded new mines on the Hills, where lumps of charcoal lay on the floors. On some days inside the caves it grew so dark we were crawling in a darkness so black that we could not see one another. I once climbed to the Upper Cave on the Male Hill with Alec Campbell and one of the National Museum drivers. We ascended without any problem, but that's only half the journey. When it was about time to go down, the driver froze. It appeared too steep. He was so scared that Alec had to go back up and rescue him. Back at camp, he faced the jokes and teasing with a smile, and such events and memories—as much as the archaeological skills and techniques—are part of what Tsodilo is all about.

Fig. 7.28 (right) & 7.29 (above): "I especially liked the geometric paintings which are painted with white pigment." Grace Babutsi saw these white geometric designs in Upper Male Hill Cave. A somewhat similar painted design occurs in South Africa near the confluence of the Limpopo and Shashe rivers.

Life in camp—as the only female member of a male team—gave me an opportunity to realize how caring our male counterparts can be. Contrary to outside expectations, I was given all the attention; they did most of the work in camp; and my small contributions were highly appreciated. I have learned so much from their wisdom; most of the experience I have is due to the participation and mentoring I received during the Tsodilo field expeditions.

I am equally indebted to both groups of villagers. They proved helpful, welcoming, cooperative, and eager to learn from what they termed "Makgowa," meaning white people. In particular, Samutjau Mukate, the chief of the Hambukushu, and C'untae Gcau, of the Juc'hoansi group, worked with the team long before the Hills were widely known. Some of the Tsodilo community members also enjoyed guiding tourists who visited the Hills, following Kefilwe Katunda, the first volunteer to do that job.

Having been a member of one of the most famous researcher teams in the world made me feel very proud; I am equally honored to have worked at Botswana's first World Heritage Site. The designation showed that people who worked at Tsodilo had produced a report that convinced the world about the importance of Tsodilo Hills. I was proud to be a woman among men, and they treated me with the respect and camaraderie they would show each other. Yet there's still room for "female bonding" in this discipline, room for the lucky women who may enrich and enliven the hard work and disciplined play of field archaeology.

~ Grace Babutsi

The Politics of Cohabitation:
Social History of Tsodilo

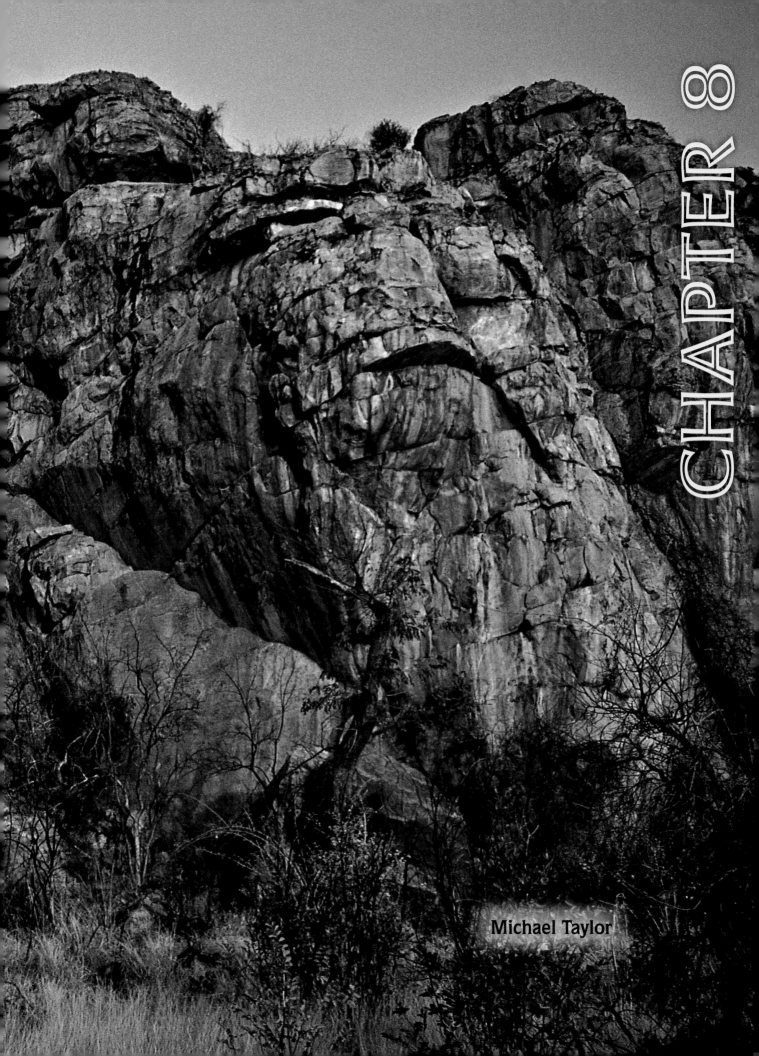

CHAPTER 8

Michael Taylor

No one knows with certainty the names and identities of those who left their marks on the stone faces of Tsodilo, but the clues they left in the archaeological record suggest they were ancestors of the people known today as San, the original inhabitants of the southern African subcontinent.

What's more, the oral histories of today's inhabitants combined with written records of nineteenth-century visitors reveal a fascinating story of human interaction, a story that hints at the pivotal role Tsodilo played in the centuries-old political and social dynamics of the northern Kalahari.

Today, two extended families call Tsodilo home, the Bantu-speaking Hambukushu and the San-speaking Juc'hoansi. At the end of the twentieth century, Samutjau (**figs. 0.4 & 8.2**) led the former; Gcau (**fig. 0.5**) led the latter. Both men were born in about 1919, and while Gcau died in 2000, Samutjau, though blind, remains active. In the mid 1800s Samutjau's great-great-grand-mother arrived at the Hills from Kavango in present-day southern Angola. Like his family today, his ancestors were cattle keepers. They moved to Tsodilo to escape a feud, taking a few cattle and supplementing their diet with wild food. Gcau's ancestors were hunter-gatherers, moving within a defined *nqore* (territory) as they followed the annual cycles of wild fruit and wildlife migrations. Their *nqore* was further south, but to escape the brutality of Batawana cattle keepers

Fig. 8.2 (above):
Samutjau Mukate, leader of the Hambukushu.

Fig. 8.1 (preceding page):
The rugged cliffs of Female Hill have provided canvases for paintings, specularite for adornment and, in the nineteenth century, a place where Ncaekhoe could defend themselves when harassed by Batawana.

who were forcing some San into servitude, they decided—around the same time as Samutjau's ancestors arrived at Tsodilo 150 years ago—to base their annual movement around Tsodilo.

Upon their arrival neither found Tsodilo empty. To the contrary, for a thousand or more years it had been inhabited by another San group, the Ncaekhoe. The story of the relationship of these three groups with one another, and with Tsodilo, speaks of larger patterns of interaction between the peoples of southern Africa and their lands, particularly that of San and Bantu-speakers.

The People of Western Ngamiland

The ancestors of the San have inhabited southern Africa for at least forty thousand years, and were likely the only residents of the subcontinent until about two thousand years ago, when Bantu-speaking agriculturalists began arriving from Central Africa. Initially, they lived on roughly equal terms with their neighbors, intermarrying and trading crops and livestock for hunted and gathered food.

Ngamiland politics changed considerably after the arrival of the Batawana in 1795. They came to Ngamiland as a small group of refugees, fleeing a leadership dispute in the Ngwato tribe in the eastern central area of what is now Botswana. For their first fifty years here the Batawana remained small and dispersed, but from 1850 they began building a strong and centralized kingdom, incorporating subject tribes into their political system. They developed a rigidly hierarchical structure, in which less politically organized tribes exchanged allegiance for a place on the ladder.

At the ladder's bottom rungs were the San, with no political rights and no payment for forced labor. San subjugation was widespread but, according to early travelers, most brutal in Ngamiland. In these turbulent times, at Tsodilo, our story begins.

Tsodilo: The Last San Outpost

Like many San groups on the northern fringes of the Kalahari, the Ncaekhoe were tall and dark. Their ancestors were Bantu-speakers who had migrated centuries earlier into Ngamiland. They had adopted a Khoesan language, but one completely different from the Juc'hoansi from western Ngamiland, Namibia, and southern Angola. They are remembered as fearless people who hunted elephants with spears, a reputation that neither the Juc'hoansi nor the Hambukushu could boast.

By the late nineteenth century the Batawana kingdom had subjugated San throughout the region, with one exception: the Ncaekhoe of Tsodilo. At that time the Ncaekhoe still "owned" the Hills, according to passed-down memory and confirmed by the journals of Siegfried Passarge, a German prospector undertaking a geological survey of Ngamiland in June 1896 and November 1898. How could the San hold out here and nowhere else? Passarge offered a clue, writing that Tsodilo "allowed some measure of political independence [to San] with withdrawing into isolated rockveld islands during the dry season rather than being stuck to permanent waterholes dominated by Bantu and Khoe."

With Tsodilo as their stronghold, the Ncaekhoe also claimed land thirty-five kilometers to the east, at a Delta lagoon, Tamatshaa, where they traded, hunted, fished, and gathered during the dry season. It is said that for generations the Ncaekhoe lived here with an intimate knowledge of the Hills, whose place names today echo their presence.

Even after 130 years, inhabitants still recall the brave words and acts of Ncaekhoe defiance. "Those arriving in this land [i.e., the Batawana] should be the ones bringing tribute to those they found here," said one Ncaekhwe leader, challenging not just the system of authority that the Batawana had set up, which demanded tribute from subject tribes, but the moral universe on which this authority rested. Such obstinacy did not go unpunished; in about 1881, Moremi II, Chief of the Batawana, dispatched a regiment to kill the Ncaekhwe leader. But the Ncaekhwe people remained, and retained control of the Hills until the early twentieth century, making Tsodilo the last stronghold of uncontested Khoisan land ownership in Ngamiland.

Arrival of Juc'hoansi and Hambukushu at Tsodilo

Individual acts of defiance aside, Tsodilo was a haven not only of reliable food and water, but also of relative peace and tranquility. Elsewhere in Ngamiland lay danger and strife. The Lozi Empire was expanding to the northeast; slave trading and despotic rulers raged in the north; and refugees fled south, where the Batawana were consolidating their power.

The Juc'hoansi at Tsodilo trace their ancestry to the region between Nxaunxau and Qangwa. They were politically independent, and economically involved in glass bead trading networks between the San and the Hambukushu. With the encroachment of Tawana hegemony into the Juc'hoansi domain, people recall stories of brutal coerced servitude for hunting and herding; those who did not obey were tied up in bundles of dry grass and set alight. Some Juc'hoansi escaped to the few remaining areas beyond Tawana direct control. One of those places was Tsodilo.

Fig. 8.4 (above):
The Juc'hoansi village near White Paintings Shelter, about 1970. Before 1970, the Juc'hoansi were fairly mobile, building their villages near water and wild food. After 1969, they settled permanently at Tsodilo and established this village. Twenty-five years later, they and their newly-acquired livestock moved to the new borehole south of the fence.

Because they were traditionally semi-nomadic, the Juc'hoansi did not settle permanently in the Hills, but migrated around the pans and fossil river valleys in the area. They commonly camped during the dry winters at Tsodilo, to take advantage of the perennial water sources and abundance of wild fruit and game there, cooking where the Site Museum now stands.

As the Juc'hoansi escaped here from encroaching despots in the east, twenty Hambukushu fled here from warlords in the north. Gibbons, an early traveler, confirmed in his journal that, during this time, "a constant stream of people fled southward to Ngamiland to come under the rule of the Tawana for their own protection."

Tsodilo's Hambukushu trace their family back to refugees from the Kavango rule of two powerful Hambukushu chiefs, Mbungu and Kathimana, chiefs who are remembered for their despotic behavior; for appropriating their subjects' property at will; for restricting trade and wealth to the chiefs and headmen; and for selling their own people to slave traders from Angola.

Samutjau's elderly aunt, Njira, who has now passed away, related how their flight from Kavango began with the clan's top hunters, Dcukiri and Djwakoba, following an elephant they had hunted and wounded. After many miles the pachyderm crossed a river at the boundary of their land and died near a village. The hunters crossed after it and met with the village chief, who agreed to share the meat. During the times of feasting, the chief also asked Djwakoba to share his sister, Moengere, as his wife. The families allowed it, but after the feast short-tempered

Djwakoba demanded her back. When the neighboring chief refused, Djwakoba crossed the river, kidnapped her in secret, then fled with his brother, sister, mother, and family southward, pursued through Tawana lands, then to Hondonga, then toward the Xeidum Valley, until finally settling at Tsodilo.

They first settled at Female Hill near a permanent water source in the cliff known as Tshokgam, cleared fields, and surrounded their village with thorn brush fences. They left several gaps in the fence, dug deep pits in them, then covered and disguised the pits with branches to trap animals that tried to enter their fields to graze. Traces of these pits remain visible today.

There are eighteenth-century Hambukushu pottery sherds, indicating that others from their tribe may have lived at Tsodilo a century earlier. Yet when they arrived, they found only the equally new Juc'hoansi arrivals and the current inhabitants, the Ncaekhoe.

Ncaekhoe, Juc'hoansi, and Hambukushu Together at Tsodilo

Despite their fierce reputation and the mutual unintelligibility of the differing clans' languages the Ncaekhoe are remembered as welcoming. Perhaps they all felt affinity against a common powerful enemy, the Batawana. The Juc'hoansi today credit the Ncaekhoe with sheltering their ancestors from Batawana raiding parties, showing them hiding places, permanent and temporary water sources, and areas rich in wild food, as well as sites of legendary significance.

There may have been translators. The Ncaekhoe knew Hambukushu from the Okavango river and knew Juc'hoansi from trade networks: they traded furs, horns, meat, ostrich feathers and eggshells, and salt from the Xeidum Valley, in return for tobacco, iron products, and grain. Hunting and gathering were among the primary means of subsistence for all three groups of people, and activities in which there was considerable co-operation. The immigrants' two star hunters were given Ncaekhoe names—Dcukuri and Djwakoba—their original Tjimukushu names now forgotten. Intermarriage sealed the ties. The "headman" Passarge met at Tsodilo was the son of a Ncaekhoe man and a Juc'hoansi woman, who had grown up in Caecae. Samutjau's grandfather, Mareka, chose a Juc'hoansi woman as a second wife. So occupants and immigrants all lived on relatively equal terms. The name Mareka was also referred to as "mother" in a prayer for rain (page 40). It should be noted that Hambukushu naming traditions, in certain instances, allow for the same name to be used for a man or woman.

The Hambukushu Move to the River

The Hambukushu lived at Tsodilo for about a generation, but still made regular trading trips to the western edge of the Delta and grew familiar with the area around Tamatshaa, the dry season camp of the Ncaekhoe. Unlike most San, their ethnic status allowed them to be granted land in return for political allegiance to the Batawana. They agreed to this alliance, presenting Chief Sekgoma Letsholathebe (1891 to 1906) with a tribute of springhare skins. In return, Letsholathebe "gave" them Tamatshaa, not recognizing any right of the Ncaekhoe to own this area.

Having stepped above the first rung of the ethno-political ladder, the Hambukushu moved from Tsodilo to Tamatshaa. Yet they did not abandon Tsodilo. Life at the river was initially very hard. They had few crops and no livestock; wild foods continued to be the primary source of nutrition. An essential element of their subsistence was the annual visits to Tsodilo for several weeks or months to collect and replenish stocks of wild fruit, especially mongongo. This was not an uncommon strategy, as observed by Nettelton generally of the Hambukushu in Ngamiland in the 1920s: "When there is wild fruit to be had, they remove into the bush where they live until the fruit is exhausted." The Juc'hoansi often camped with the Hambukushu on these visits, assisting them in collecting fruit and hunting, and then returning with them to Tamatshaa to be given items such as axe-heads, clay pots, and tobacco.

The Ncaekhoe Abandon Tsodilo

After they had lived together for several decades, tensions between the Juc'hoansi and Ncaekhoe began to grow. It is not clear what caused the tensions—perhaps the pressure and stress of sharing the low-yielding permanent water sources during the dry season. Nevertheless, in the early years of the twentieth century, the Ncaekhoe left Tsodilo. Why depart after centuries of control? The Juc'hoansi today recall their parting as amicable:

> The Ncaekhoe, our in-laws, then started becoming afraid of us. They told us, "Yes, our in-laws, you see this land here—it is yours. We are leaving it for you. Take it. We also fear you because you have poisoned arrows. You are our in-laws, so we are leaving this land for you, live in it." So we lived in it.

First the Ncaekhoe moved more permanently to Tamatshaa Lagoon on the Delta's edge, land that was no longer regarded as their own since the Batawana chieftainship had granted it to Samutjau's ancestors. Oral history is confirmed by the record of an early traveler, Franz Seiner, who on a trip up the western edge of the Okavango Delta in 1907 met the Ncaekhoe at a temporary village at Tamatshaa. The departure of the Ncaekhoe from Tsodilo created a political vacuum that the Batawana-allied Hambukushu quickly filled. Hunting rights to the fertile hunting grounds around Tsodilo fell to Samutjau's ancestors, and soon their roughly egalitarian bond with the Juc'hoansi degenerated into the patron-client relationship so common elsewhere.

Stratification did not reduce interaction between the Hambukushu and the Juc'hoansi, but irrevocably changed it. They still foraged and hunted together, but this food grew less critical than cattle, which the Hambukushu owned but the Juc'hoansi herded and milked. Once equipped with horse and gun, Samutjau's reliance on the San decreased, along with their share of meat.

Water, of course, held much of life and politics in the balance.

Samutjau granted a Herero named Kahube permission in 1951 to set up a cattle post at Tsodilo; and though the well he dug on the old lake floor yielded sufficient water, his cows became sick and after several years he abandoned it. Cattle fared better at Tamatshaa, along the river, until overgrazing the fodder into scarcity prompted the Hambukushu to once again set their sights on Tsodilo. In 1959, Samutjau and a Lozi man moved back to Tsodilo with several horses and donkeys to repair and deepen Kahube's well. After scraping and digging by hand through the many meters of calcrete, they found success. The next year Samutjau moved with his family and livestock back to Tsodilo, building their village on the old lakebed west of Male Hill, the present site of the airstrip. When this flooded they moved up onto the sand ridge, where the village remains today. The baobabs, ivory palms, and marula trees in the village that have now grown large were planted by Samutjau's father.

Tsodilo Opens Up to the Outside World

Although there were a significant number of visitors to Tsodilo from the 1950s onward, one in particular brought it out of obscurity forever: Laurens van der Post (**fig. 8.5**).

In 1955, van der Post's dream of the "wild bushmen" of the Kalahari took him to the western side of the Okavango Delta, where he met "Samutshoso" (Samutjau), who brought the Afrikaner author to Tsodilo, hoping to find the Juc'hoansi there. They missed the San by a week, but did "discover" some rock paintings, as well as experience inexplicable problems with their camera equipment. This culminated in van der Post making his team sign a letter of apology addressed to "The Spirits,"

Fig. 8.5 (left):
Laurens van der Post at Tsodilo.

which he put in a bottle and placed beside a prominent panel on the Female Hill. He immortalized his experiences at Tsodilo in his 1958 classic, *The Lost World of the Kalahari* (**fig. 8.6**), in which he poetically described Tsodilo as "a great fortress of once living Bushmen culture, a Louvre of the desert filled with treasure."

Fig. 8.6 (above):
Laurens van der Post's classic book, The Lost World of the Kalahari, *enlarged and reprinted in 1988.*

The steady increase in numbers of visitors boosted Samutjau's status and fortunes as a guide, and persuaded the Juc'hoansi to settle more permanently at Tsodilo. The visitors brought opportunities to earn a small income, as related by Gcau:

> In the past, we were just living here, not anticipating that eventually there would be large numbers of white people coming here. In those days if we saw a white person we would run away because they were unfamiliar to us. They would call us, "No, come here, I have come here to visit you." When we overcame our fear, we began showing them around the paintings. From there, white people started coming one by one, coming to see the paintings. This was before Samutjau had come here, he was still at Tamatshaa. When we had shown them around, they would give us food and we would eat and be satisfied, and we would all be happy, us and the white people.

Gcau and his family settled several kilometers away from Samutjau's village, growing sedentary through acquisition of cattle in the 1980s, as payment for herding and donated by the government.

While the Hills themselves remain timeless, the increasing global interest in Tsodilo has placed a new set of demands on the area and on its inhabitants. The Hambukushu and Juc'hoansi families had to struggle to maintain a sense of control over the area they regard as their own, but at the same time find new opportunities to earn an income and praise from sharing their knowledge of the Hills with visitors.

Equality and Inequality at Tsodilo Today

The Hambukushu and Juc'hoansi who live at Tsodilo today have developed a relationship that has spanned several generations of close contact, a relationship that reflects the wider dynamics between the San and Bantu-speakers in southern Africa. Although equality is enshrined in the constitution and laws of Botswana, the heritage of the Juc'hoansi as hunter-gatherers still today gives their ethnicity a stigma in the eyes of many of their non-San neighbors. This has real implications for land rights.

Samutjau simply echoed popular sentiment when he explained that,

> "Mosarwa [a San person] is just a thing that does not care for owning land. They just move around following animals. This land around Tsodilo is all mine."

Needless to say, the Juc'hoansi at Tsodilo tend to differ with that opinion. In the words of Gcau:

> We used to be alone on this land. There were no black people. After meeting Batswana in the times of MmaMosadinyana [Queen Victoria] we met Hambukushu. They were not very powerful as they did not have guns. They tried to tell us this was their land. From there the government came in and the Hambukushu told them this was their land, and the government agreed. Now when things are done we are not listened to. We are not taken as people. No one listens to us. He [Samutjau] is the chief, but that chief does not explain to anyone how he became chief, and he doesn't tell anything to those people he found on the land. He tells us we have no power, we have nothing, he must be chief. About those he found here when he first came to Tsodilo, he says, "They are just 'Basarwa,'" and has no respect for them.

Yet, despite this tension, the two families are in many ways interdependent. Whereas in the distant past the San may have been respected, even feared, because of their use of the deadly poison from the *Diamphidia simplex* beetle they used on their arrowheads, today familiarity can sometimes breed contempt. "The Hambukushu are not afraid of us because they know us well. Fear comes from not knowing," commented C'untae, Gcau's son **(fig. 0.8)**. In these close networks are strands of tension that arise from the dominant position that the Hambukushu invariably have in the different aspects of their interrelationship.

Both families take part in meetings called by the Government, District Council, and Museum. There they stand on equal terms regarding language, as they are conducted in one foreign to them all—Setswana. However, in the larger meetings attended by outside officials, the Juc'hoansi generally keep quiet and the discussion is done by the Hambukushu. When asked why this is so, the Juc'hoansi claim they are ridiculed if they try to contribute, as it is not their place to speak in such meetings.

Many of the important rituals are shared by the two families. As commented upon by Njira, one of the old Hambukushu women, the sharing of these rituals and daily aspects of their lives breeds and strengthens familiarity and closeness; "We give birth together, so how can we not get along with each other?" Such a relationship does not necessarily imply equality, however. Funerals, for example, involve the active participation of members of both villages, although the roles played in the funeral ceremony vary according to which village the deceased called home. In Juc'hoansi funerals, Hambukushu commonly share the key roles, such as the leading of prayers, with the Juc'hoansi. In Hambukushu funerals, however, the Juc'hoansi play a more passive role, while the key functions are again performed by the Hambukushu themselves.

In rituals of healing, as well, the Juc'hoansi and Hambukushu are brought together. The Juc'hoansi at Tsodilo no longer perform trance dances **(fig. 8.7)**, even though several of the elderly men know how. The fact that none of the younger generation knows how to enter a trance as part of the healing dance indicates that for several decades the Juc'hoansi have primarily sought elsewhere for the healing of physical ailments, and have relied largely on other means for maintaining social cohesion. Some Juc'hoansi do partake in trance dances, but this is done at Cobasha, where there are Juc'hoansi who regularly do so. Juc'hoansi treat minor ailments themselves, but for most major cases of sickness Samutjau, who has a great reputation as a healer, is consulted by Juc'hoansi and Hambukushu alike. For this he is usually paid between five pula (US$0.75) and several hundred pula, in cash or in kind, depending on the seriousness of the sickness and his success in healing it. The District Health Team visits Tsodilo monthly, and is generally used if other attempts at healing have been unsuccessful.

The rise in tourism and the resources this brings to Tsodilo have only added new dimensions to an already long-evolved and multilayered relationship between the Juc'hoansi and the Hambukushu of Tsodilo. It is a relationship in which they have many common interests, but in which there are also tensions arising from opposing and competing claims and a legacy of ethnic inequalities. ■

Fig. 8.7 (above):
A Juc'hoansi healing dance at Tsodilo, about 1995. Women and children sit around a specially-lighted fire, sing and clap special songs, while men dance, circling around them. Here, Gcau leads the line of dancers. Some dancers will enter a trance and heal fragile community relations and sickness. Many Hambukushu recognise the benefits gained and attend dances, usually sitting by the fire, but sometimes joining the dancers. With the passing of the elder San at Tsodilo, the dances are no longer practised there. Some researchers believe rock paintings may be attempts to portray their trance experiences.

Absorbing Change:
Tsodilo Today

**Michael Taylor
and Alec Campbell**

When UNESCO listed Tsodilo as a World Heritage Site, global recognition had local repercussions. The eldest members of the two long-standing communities of the Hills have witnessed the trickle of intrepid 1950s explorers become an ephemeral stream of visitors in the 1980s who now arrive in an annual flood of ten thousand tourists.

However, this outside exposure is but the most visible force and facet of change in recent decades; others have been taking place beneath the surface.

The People of Tsodilo and Their Lives

In 1959, when Samutjau and his family moved permanently back to Tsodilo from the river at Tamatshaa, his herd numbered fifteen head of cattle and a few goats (**fig. 9.2**). By 1996, when Botswana slaughtered all Ngamiland cattle to curb lung disease, Samutjau had built his herd to four hundred. This slaughter brought a huge cash injection into his village; only one quarter of the cattle were replaced, while the government compensated for the rest with cash at 500 pula per head. Samutjau's family is now slowly rebuilding their herd back to its previous levels. At roughly the same time the Juc'hoansi at Tsodilo also received a huge cash injection; a small portion to compensate for the thirty cattle they owned while the bulk, 17,000 pula, was for relocating their village.

Perhaps the biggest change was the fact that the Juc'hoansi had a permanent village to relocate in the first place. Until the 1970s, they moved semi-nomadically around different parts of their territory, including Tsodilo, depending on the availability of water and wild foods, wildlife movements, and work opportunities as cattle herders. Their dependence on wildlife declined as laws grew ever more restrictive, from allowing unlimited hunting prior to the Unified Hunting Regulations of 1979, to allowing no subsistence hunting at all for the Juc'hoansi at Tsodilo after 1997. Several Juc'hoansi households now own about forty cattle, most given to them under a government program to encourage former hunter-gatherers to "sedentarize" by replacing hunting with livestock rearing.

Hambukushu men (but no Juc'hoansi from Tsodilo) used to join men from all over southern Africa as migrant laborers in the South African mines, but no longer. Some residents seek income from Tsodilo visitors, employment, guiding, and selling of crafts; most people must rely on their own resources.

Fig. 9.1 (preceding page):
Samutjau transporting water by ox-drawn sledge from his well before the National Museum drilled a borehole close to his village.

Fig. 9.2 (right):
In 1964, both Hambukushu and Juc'hoansi drew water from a six-meter pit dug just north of the Rhino Panel. The Hambukushu owned few cattle and the Juc'hoansi had none. Here, Samutjau stands among his small herd; water is bailed from the pit, passed upwards in buckets and poured into a wooden trough where only two animals at a time were allowed to drink.

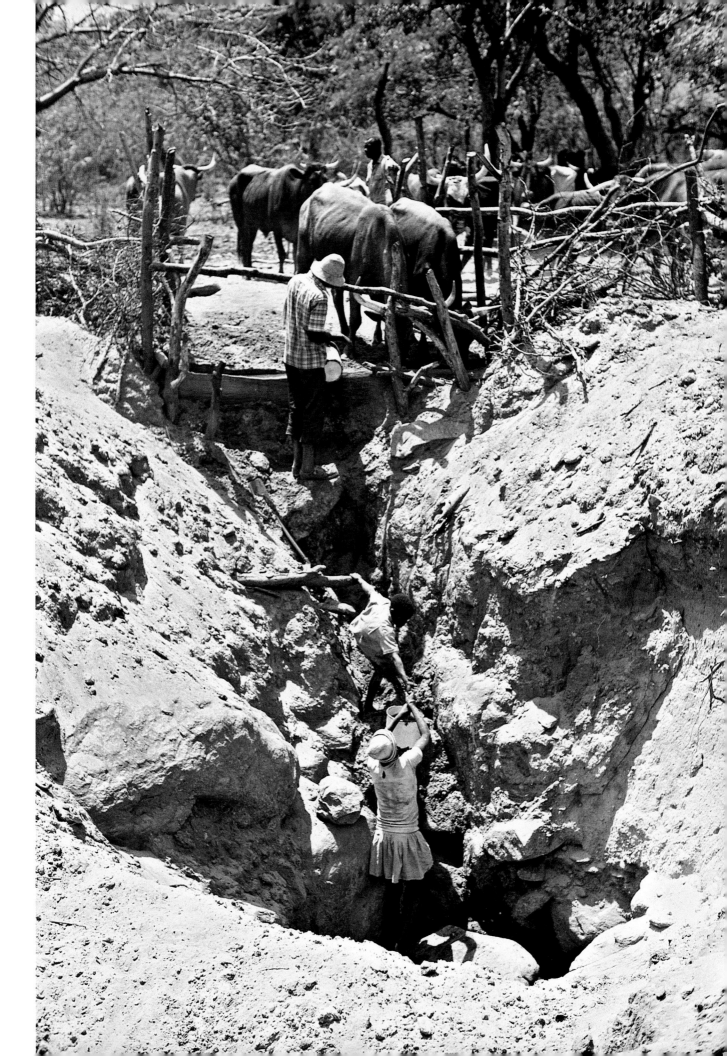

Crop production is a possibility in years of good rain, but rain's unpredictability makes it a less and less attractive option. The Hambukushu may plant only a fraction of their forty-five hectares of cleared fields; the Juc'hoansi generally plant none of the 1.5 hectares that the government has marked out as their communal field. Instead, both villages continue to rely on Tsodilo's abundant wild food, including fruits, berries, rhizomes, bulbs, nuts, green leaves, flying ants, and caterpillars—food that endures when drought kills cultivated sources. Perhaps the most nutritious, mongongo tree nuts grow abundant on the Hills' eastern sand ridges. The Hambukushu brew *mogwana* (*Grewia bicolor*) into a wine known as *khadi* and sell it to the Juc'hoansi.

Fig. 9.3 (above):
MmaMukate with grewia berries she has collected near the north end of Female Hill. She sells some of the berries for cash and keeps some to brew mogwana, *an alcoholic drink, mainly for home consumption, but also for sale.*

Government welfare is so prevalent that many worry about the dependency it breeds. Most households receive one of the following: drought relief; old-age pensions; or food packages for orphans, lactating mothers, tuberculosis patients, children under five, and those classed as destitute.

Village Infrastructure

Roughly 120 Hambukushu and 50 Juc'hoansi inhabit Tsodilo, up from 50 and 20, respectively, three decades back, and showing growth rates slightly above national average. The Hambukushu settlement nearest Male Hill consists of scattered, reed-fenced courtyards, each with two to five round houses made of pole-and-mud walls with thatched roofs. Surrounding these are a number of bush-fenced cattle byres. The Juc'hoansi settlement, on the sand ridge several kilometers west of the Male Hill, is of similar construction, but more compact (**fig. 9.4**).

Tsodilo falls eighty people short of the government rule that would qualify it as a "village," with rights to facilities such as a government-drilled borehole, a school, and a clinic. The National Museum provided a borehole to supplement two existing hand-dug wells that slake the thirst of Hambukushu cattle. That borehole and a building for the mobile clinic are the only government infrastructure; there is no piped water, electricity, or other facilities.

The lack of a local school leaves three in four adults illiterate; their children must be educated elsewhere. Hambukushu children move near river villages to live with relatives, while adult Juc'hoansi with their children must move to Nxaunxau, 45 kilometers to the southwest, where they also stay with relatives, returning to Tsodilo only on the holidays.

Visions of the Future for Tsodilo

As residents of Tsodilo look eagerly toward the emerging tourist-driven future of the Hills, some elders, especially the Juc'hoansi, feel nostalgia for the past. Said Shoroka, Gcau's younger brother:

> The life we live today is that of black people, it is not our own. These changes were forced on us by black people who own the government and rule over us. They have said now that

Fig. 9.4 (above):
When the Joc'hoansi moved, they built sturdy homes, in many ways similar to houses in the Hambukushu village. They fenced their yards with wooden poles and wire to keep their livestock out. Their village is only two hundred meters from the new borehole making water for both domestic use and livestock easy to obtain, but it is nearly six kilometers from the Hills, creating a long walk to work, to sell crafts, and to gather wild food.

our culture is against the law and we cannot hunt. The government says we kill the land by hunting. But how can that be true, as when we were living with our culture the land was full of animals. Today we live by cattle, but the better life was with wild animals. In the old days we hunted and ate meat and danced, and we governed ourselves. We ate what we wanted and the animals didn't get finished. Life was better before we started living off sugar and beers.

Both the Juc'hoansi and the Hambukushu remain skeptics as to whether World Heritage Site status will reverse their sense of increasing alienation from the land and resources around Tsodilo. Kelebetse Keasheta, a young Mumbukushu, was afraid preserving Tsodilo would also preserve his settlement's crude, neglected state: "Now that this is a tourist area, we cannot have development. You can hear the noise in the distance of the generator providing the Site Museum with electricity, but here at our homes we will never get such facilities." Mokgosi Dihama, a Mumbukushu elder, was even more blunt about his fears: "The way I see it is that white people will end up taking Tsodilo for themselves."

Tsodilo carries a spectrum of meanings to diverse people over shifting epochs. For at least forty thousand years it was a center of food and water resources, a center of religious significance, an axis of mining, and an exchange for trade. For over a century the Hambukushu and the Juc'hoansi found in the Hills safe haven from oppression and an island of secure food and water. In the last few decades Tsodilo has become a tourist magnet, and now a World Heritage Site that demands conservation. Meeting the varied interests of all these diverse stakeholders is never easy, but most remain hopeful that change will bring some opportunity. As Dihama pragmatically put it, "At least when the white people come to Tsodilo I can sell them something and get a bit of money to buy soap." ■

Robert K. Hitchcock

CHAPTER 10

Rock Art Tourism:
Development through Conservation

When Botswana's *Vision 2016* aimed to enhance historical and cultural tourism, when the Department of Tourism set out to increase tourism's share of the country's gross domestic product, when the 2001 National Eco-Tourism Development Strategy tried to assist "rural communities while at the same time safeguarding natural and cultural resources," when the government sought to diversify tourism as a form of development, when promoters printed brochures, when Air Botswana laid out its flight magazines, and when leaders proposed World Heritage Sites for inclusion on UNESCO's elite list of cultural, historical, natural, and artistic places, all these planners must have had one common place in mind: Tsodilo Hills.

With such powerful interests behind it, Tsodilo's stature would inevitably rise to its rightful place in the world. Yet just as surely these very same interests would find it hard to agree on exactly where that place would be, what it would look like, who would benefit from it, and how to run it.

The early risk, of neglect, gave way to a bigger risk: that it might be smothered by competing kinds of love. Modern officials and resource managers would have to collaborate as skillfully and intricately as the inhabitants who have lived and worked here side by side over the millennia.

Integrated Approaches

The first strategic approach was basic: Should we conserve Tsodilo for its inherent legacy or develop it for the modern human economy? The answer, as it turned out, was both. Two progressive management plans, drafted in 1994 and 2005 by the National Museum and a regional reference group, respectively, integrated conservation and development strategies for long-term sustainability.

Fig. 10.1 (preceding page):
Looking south from Divuyu plateau towards Male Hill and the flat Kalahari. Divuyu Trail passes to the left of the foreground rocks and descends into the valley joining Rhino Trail where sun and shadow meet. Together the trails descend into the lower valley with Snake Mine and Rhino Panel under the rocks at the base of the small hill. Hambukushu fields can be seen on the plain.

Fig. 10.2 (right):
Xauwe using a red-hot wire to incise an antelope's outline into a piece of tomato-box. After drawing more animals on the plank, he will sell it to tourists for perhaps ten or twenty pula.

The National Museum and the Trust for Okavango Cultural and Development Initiatives (TOCaDI) initiated a planning process that took into consideration all of Tsodilo's stakeholders and interest groups. Stakeholders include anthropologists, archaeologists, and artists like Sue Bucklin who have been involved in activities in the Hills since at least the early 1960s. They also include the National Museum, Monuments, and Art Gallery of Botswana that in the 1970s began an extensive rock art and archaeological site recording effort. They include Botswana development workers, NGOs (non-governmental organizations), and consulting groups hired to help promote social and economic development in the Hills. Above all, they include Tsodilo's residents, who have seen their socioeconomic statuses expand and contract over time, depending upon government and district policies, numbers of visitors, drought conditions, and local development work.

Certain stakeholders have emphatically different interpretations of "development" and "conservation." Consider livestock. One man's four-legged bank account, milk supply, or bride wealth is another man's destructive, noxious, invasive alien species. In the 1990s some tourists, seeking peace and inspiration at Tsodilo, complained that cattle and goats "wreaked havoc, eating sleeping bags and clothing and kicking over pots and pans." Land use planning sought to anticipate, resolve and reduce such conflicts in advance.

The planning process also sought to answer the question: Who should benefit from the presence of the rock art and culturally significant places at Tsodilo? The San here value art as a central focus of their existence, their traditions, and their belief systems and spirituality, from hunting to water to trance dancing. The Hambukushu also have close ties to the art and archaeology here, engaging in rituals in some of the caves and using local materials for healing and other purposes. Clearly, both local groups had a sense of ownership and belonging both stronger and older than that of any other stakeholders.

Yet they are not alone in deserving a seat at the table. Rock art is found in other areas of Botswana, as well, but nowhere else in the country are paintings so numerous, diverse, and extensive. It is the teams of

explorer archaeologists who helped put the place on the global map and who continue to unlock and interpret its meaning and significance to outsiders. Likewise, substantial investments in time, money, training, energy, and other resources have come from distant stakeholders, many of whom have never set eyes on Tsodilo Hills. All these stakeholders—scholars, residents, taxpayers, donors, foundations, governments, the Tsodilo Hills Community Trust, and the National Museum—were integrated into one overarching group, the Tsodilo Hills Management Authority.

Land Use Planning, Development, and Tourism in Tsodilo

Authority means little without direction or a blueprint. That blueprint began to take shape from the start, when Tsodilo's paintings were gazetted as a national monument in 1937 under the Bushmen Relics Act, even before Botswana was a nation-state. Later, the Tsodilo Hills were gazetted under the Ngamiland District Land Use Plan as NG 6, which has an area of 225 square kilometers. It was zoned as a photographic safari area, an area for environmentally and culturally oriented tourism. In a nation renowned for tourism sites, Tsodilo has competition—Savute's rock art and wildlife in the Chobe National Park, for example—but no other areas have earned the attention, recognition, and financial and development investment that the Hills have received.

Some claim that these investments seldom trickle down to the local Hambukushu and Juc'hoansi villages, whose members primarily earn their livelihoods through diversified strategies, including foraging and hunting with craft production and sale; keeping livestock; and, in some cases, growing crops. Yet there are benefits. Old San may receive pensions; others get handouts from the National Destitutes Policy, and both San and Hambukushu have been employed by Botswana's labor-based public works program, building roads for cash wages. Recently some have been trained to improve their knowledge and skills as interpretive guides at Tsodilo, in anticipation of the tourists who are arriving in increasing numbers.

Interviews with Tsodilo's residents indicate that they appreciate the tourists in general, except for the careless ones who drive off-road, build wasteful bonfires, and spray water and soft drinks on paintings to make a glossier photograph. Conversely, some tourists have complained that the San and Hambukushu here do not know very much about the rock art or about how to deal with visitors. Local peoples recognize this as a problem, and have eagerly sought more and more advanced guide training. They see tourists, and the cultural resources here, as both their birthright and their responsibility. They want more knowledge, more advanced guide training, more locally driven preservation for the future, and better tourism brochures that both enhance understanding and address appropriate ways for tourists to behave with respect to the rock art, people, and environment.

Craft Production and Income Generation

Guiding is not the only way locals benefit from tourism. The Gantsi Craft Marketing Company conducted a workshop to improve the quality and marketing of local arts and crafts that draw their inspiration from the art in Tsodilo. Handmade seed necklaces and greeting cards are now sold at Tsodilo's site museum, which provides income to local producers.

The Juc'hoansi also manufacture and sell ostrich eggshell bead necklaces and other crafts. However modest these seem, a 1990 survey showed these sales represented a third to a half of their annual income—income they reinvested in livestock, clothing, blankets, and food, and income they spend on school uniforms in order to send their children to schools in Shakawe and elsewhere in Botswana.

As we've seen, people at Tsodilo have produced and traded ostrich eggshell beads for tens of thousands of years, but never before on such a commercial scale. Some worried the resource was not sustainable. This may be a valid concern. The San and Hambukushu here use a wide variety of natural resources in craft production

Table 10.1: *Natural Resources Used for Craft Production by Juc'hoan and Mbukushu in the Northwestern Kalahari Desert Region, Botswana*

Scientific Name	Juc'hoan Name	Part Utilized	Products Made
Acacia tortilis	/aqri	root	quivers
Boscia albitrunca	zaqn	stem	animal/human figurines, spoons
Burkea africana	!ku	stem	drums, thumb piano bases
Colophospermum mopane	mophane	stem	bracelets, rings, walking sticks, animals
Combretum apiculatum	//aqean	stem	etched plaques
Combretum imberbe	/'o	stem	figurines, spoons
Commiphora spp.	mokomoto or seroka depending on species	stem	animals, figurines, drums
Gardenia resiniflua	morala	stem	spoons, bowls
Grewia flava	n/ang	branch	bows, digging sticks
Kirkia acuminata	modumela	stem	figurines, candle holders, toy chairs
Lonchocarpus nelsii	//'haoh	stem	figurines, spoons
Phragmites australis	//'ang/'o	branch	arrows
Pterocarpus angolensis	n/hang	stem	drums, thumb piano bases, plaques
Ricinodendron rautanenii	g//kaa	stem (trunk)	stools
Sansevieria scabrifolia	g!oma	leaves	snares, mats, bow strings
Sclerocarya birrea	kaqe, morula	stem (trunk)	bowls, pestles, plaques
Terminalia sericea	za'o	stem	etched plaques

Fig. 10.3 (below):
The Museum shop at the reception center. The Museum sells crafts made by Tsodilo residents on their behalf at no profit to itself—baskets, decorated bags, wooden bowls and dishes, bows and arrows, seed jewelry, and dolls in traditional dress.

Fig. 10.4 (left):
Selling seed necklaces for cash, 1995. Today,
for some Tsodilo residents, sale of curios can
provide half or even more of their cash incomes.

Fig. 10.5 (above):
Making ostrich eggshell beads using a length of fencing wire
ground to a fine point. Long ago, the same beads were made using
a carefully pointed piece of quartz or chert also mounted in a stick.

(table 10.1). Most resources are widely available, but there are limited amounts of the kinds of plants, wood, or other resources used in craft production. One role for the Tsodilo Hills Management Authority is to help people quantify resources here and establish quotas for managing them.

The Ostrich Eggshell Problem

A good starting place might be the surprisingly pivotal egg of the ostrich (*Struthio camelus*). In the past, the Juc'hoansi foraged for eggs as food, using empty shells as canteens to carry water. Both women and men decorate whole ostrich eggs by carving designs on them with pointed tools. Women work broken eggshell pieces into beads, the exchange of which has linked people in a complex system of mutual reciprocity across the region. People in Tsodilo wear necklaces from as far away as Caecae in the south, Nyae Nyae to the west, and Kapatura in the Caprivi Strip to the north. Chapter 3 revealed that ostrich eggshell beads have been made and used at Tsodilo for at least 27,000 years.

However, since 1994 problems have arisen. Botswana established an Ostrich Policy under which people can't process ostrich products without a special game license (SGL) issued by the Department of Wildlife and National Parks. To get a permit, people must pay a fee; and to earn a fee they must sell crafts, like ostrich

Fig. 10.6 (above):
Qoo selling ostrich eggshell belts and pendants west of Hukuntsi Village in Northern Kgalagadi District.

shell necklaces. Even then they can collect shells only from April to August (putting them out in the field during peak tourist season) and must store the shells ready for regular inspection by the Department of Wildlife and National Parks. Rather than risk arrest, women stay home, idle. Women's groups in West Hanahai in Ghanzi District who attempted to establish ostrich user groups wasted two years, from 1993 to 1995, awaiting a permit.

One compromise proposal is that the Maiteko Tshwaragano Development Trust could serve as a repository or ostrich egg "bank," whose products could then be allocated to individuals for craft production. Yet herein lies another catch-22. A regional wildlife officer still argues that the manufacture of ostrich eggshell products by NGOs is illegal under Section 65 of the Wildlife Conservation and National Parks Act of 1992, which states, "No person other than the holder of a trophy dealer's licence shall employ or engage any other person to manufacture any article from any trophy." Special game license holders are not allowed to hold any other licenses besides their SGL, so if hatched egg pieces are indeed "trophies," women in those quiet and modest craft groups must be breaking the law.

Ironically, the same law allows harvest of ostrich eggs for food or as raw material; just not for value-added crafts. No wonder locals at Tsodilo are confused: national policy contradicts itself. Unless collectors and craft producers shall be simultaneously violating and complying with the law, unless women and men should have different rights regarding ostrich shells; unless people should not manage their own resources, the Tsodilo Hills Management Authority could help resolve this evident policy conflict to safeguard the rights of people in remote and rural areas in Botswana.

Tourism to Bring Development through Conservation

Tsodilo tourists come not only to visit the rock art sites but also to appreciate and understand the Hills' fascinating cultural and geomorphological history. As shown in this book, all three dynamics—art, people, and place—are inextricably woven together. This raises questions about decisions regarding the status and land rights of the Juc'hoansi and Hambukushu today. Were they forced off the land and resources they inhabited, or did they voluntarily move?

The answer lies at the core of the debate about tourism, and how it can reveal development versus conservation as a false dichotomy. For at Tsodilo, people had enough options and enlightened leadership to achieve development *through* conservation.

In 1993 Alec Campbell prepared an implementation project for the Tsodilo Hills Management Plan aimed at ensuring better conservation of a major rock art and archaeological landscape. This entailed attending meetings, or *kgotla*, with both communities, with the Tawana Land Board, and with the North West District Council, to decide where and how the Juc'hoansi would live. All agreed that:

- Cattle and goats had seriously overgrazed the area west of the Hills and had been seen standing in, and rubbing against, several shelters that contain low-level rock paintings.
- Their potential for damage required an east-west fence around the future wilderness area to exclude livestock yet avoid existing houses, lands, and water sources.
- The National Museum spent 250,000 pula (about US$40,000) drilling two boreholes, one for its own use on the north side of the fence, and one for public use, two kilometers west of the Mbukushu village, on the south side of the fence.
- Residents held the right to use natural resources, such as thatching grass and fruit, north of the fence.
- Controlled tourism, an integral part of the plan, was welcomed by all Tsodilo residents.
- The Juc'hoansi village would remain at the foot of Female Hill, provided they cleaned up trash and moved their livestock to a place south of the fence.

At that crucial meeting, Xauwe, on behalf of the Juc'hoansi and after some discussion, said that because the Juc'hoansi did not want to be separated from their livestock, they chose to move south of the fence, but in their own time and to a place of their own choosing. They moved over a year later, were compensated at the normal government rates, and chose to live and build their village within two hundred meters of the new community borehole. They retained the rights to their existing village and a few people either could live in it or occupy it on a daily basis during the tourist season, using it as a base for tourist activities such as photography, sale of crafts, or guiding.

In short, the Juc'hoansi chose where they wanted to live and have a borehole with clean water next to their stock kraal and within two hundred meters of their village. This is an improvement over their original village, where they had to walk a considerable distance to get water at the Hambukushu well, water that was (and is) seriously contaminated by cattle urine.

Conclusions

The Juc'hoansi were anxious to see the development of tourism at Tsodilo, but elected not to retain their original village. The National Museum has a shop at Tsodilo that sells both Juc'hoan and Hambukushu crafts at standard agreed-upon prices and at no profit to the National Museum itself. The Juc'hoansi, as the main guides, wait at the Site Museum's headquarters, the only campsite with ablution blocks and water, to act as assistants to tourists. Standard rates are paid directly to the guides.

Because of the small number of residents, Tsodilo is still classified as a cattle post, so no school has been built there. Even so, a clinic has been erected and the Medical Department, Community Development, North West District Council staff, and other development workers make regular visits.

Other problems remain intractable. Alcohol is, and always has been, brewed and sold by Tsodilo residents. The settlement's *semausu* (tiny shop) sells canned beer to anyone, including Juc'hoansi. Human immunodeficiency virus (HIV) is endemic today in Botswana and spread in Tsodilo, almost certainly, by residents returning from working abroad, by civil servant visitors, by police and the army, and by road construction workers, among others. These problems must be addressed, but are hardly the result of increased tourism.

Indeed, from the perspective of the government and of Tsodilo's residents, progress has come, offering better opportunities, largely through tourism, the only alternative to agriculture in northern Botswana. The development of Tsodilo in order to conserve a magnificent set of archaeological sites, to attract and control a burgeoning tourist industry, and to provide a means for local people to make money was seen as imperative. Any tourism success came not by accident, or inevitably, but rather through careful, painstaking discussion. This discussion assessed options for fences and boreholes, attempted to accommodate foraging and herding priorities, and included all of the residents of Tsodilo as they pondered what should be done and how it could be implemented. This discussion has involved patience and respect, has lasted for years, and, indeed, still continues to this day. ∎

ART AND THE SAN

Art is a visible and important symbol of the San in northwestern and western Botswana. Artistic expression represented a set of skills that many San possessed and upon which they could build, forging a connection between young and old, between males and females, and between those living on farms and in town and those remaining in the bush. The sale of art, including craft items such as decorated (etched) ostrich eggshells, paintings, and carved wooden items, is a means of generating much-needed income for San individuals and households, as well as a means of expressing a set of identities that are a source of pride for many San.

San value art as a central focus of their existence; crucial aspects of lifestyles and existence are recorded in art, and include the hunting of animals, the gathering of wild plants, interactions between San and other groups, the herding of livestock, and the performance of trance healing rituals.

CONTEMPORARY SAN ART: THE KURU ARTS PROJECT IN D'KAR

A 1989 visit to the Tsodilo Hills stimulated the Naro San of D'kar in Ghanzi District to undertake artistic activities. They saw art of high quality, shared their observations with their village, and helped found the Kuru Arts Project in 1990.

The project trained San artists in oil and watercolor painting, lithography, etching, and printmaking. It exhibited artists' work at museums and art galleries—from Gaborone, Windhoek, Johannesburg, and Bulawayo to London, Amsterdam, Toronto, and Albuquerque—to positive reactions and increasing demand. Some San artists even have gained a worldwide reputation; British Airways chose a painting by Cg'ose Ntcox'o to decorate its jetliners.

Fig. 10.7 (left): "Ostriches and other birds in the forest"—an oil painting by the late Dada who passed away in her 70s. Dada, whose given name is Coexae Gqam, learned to paint at Kuru, in the Ghanzi District. Her work has been exhibited around the world with one of her designs used by British Airways on the tail of a Boeing.

Of fourteen Kuru artists, five are women and nine are men, ranging in age from their early twenties to seventy-five. Kuru's artists aren't the only ones in D'kar, but they reflect a cross-section of the people involved in producing fine art. The San artists create personal symbols but also draw inspiration from the Australian Aboriginals or Native Americans. The images they create may include humans, plants, clouds with rain, birds, scorpions, praying mantises, dung beetles, spiders, and tortoise. They paint kudu, eland, giraffe, hyenas, leopards, and ostriches, which they've seen; or elephant and rhinoceros, which they haven't.

Most Kuru artists generate substantial incomes, compared to their neighbors in the Ghanzi District, and most set aside some of their funds to buy goods or food for relatives and friends. They thus become central nodes in a wide-ranging network of reciprocal exchange: the individual artist her- or himself may not become materially wealthy, but incurs obligations on the part of others, upon whom they can then call in time of need.

They generate income both from direct sale and licensing of the materials they produce. In line with the efforts of indigenous peoples worldwide to protect their intellectual property rights, the San of western Botswana have sought to ensure economic returns for the use of their images and symbols. Kuru helps secure copyrights for individuals and groups; it helps train artists from Caecae in western Ngamiland; and it helps artists price and market their products. These go beyond paintings, to musical recordings, postcards, stationery, T-shirts, or a hand-printed artists' book, *Qauqaua*, bound in goatskin tanned by D'kar leatherworkers using special roots that were carefully prepared.

Kuru's returns on investment are substantial, both in quantifiable income and in the immeasurable pride of an often marginalized people. These are people who value their environment and their social relations past and present; people linked both aesthetically and spiritually through their connective tissue, art.

~ Robert K. Hitchcock

143

The Power of Intangible Heritage:
Bottom-Up Management

CHAPTER 11

Phillip Segadika

*V*isitors quickly grasp *why* Tsodilo became Botswana's first World Heritage Site; what they rarely appreciate is *how*. That story has drama, complexities, and politics of its own.

The Tsodilo area started in bad shape. A decade ago Tsodilo was one of the region's poorest cattle posts, receiving for the number of its inhabitants, an enhanced share of government handouts, and unable to retain or educate its young. Since then the years have brought major lifestyle changes: the San relocated with their government-provided livestock; the Hambukushu's plowed fields gave way to the Botswana National Museum; the number of tourists to the area rose dramatically **(table 11.1)**; the access road was graveled and graded; a protective fence was erected around the core area of the Hills; and a small cottage industry has emerged.

Table 11.1: Visitor Statistics at Tsodilo

Year	Number of Visitors
2001	2,301
2002	3,313
2003	5,096
2004	9,510
2005	10,362

Yet the area seemed so sleepy and empty that in 2001 the International Council on Monuments and Sites (ICOMOS) advised UNESCO: "Three basic long-term facts contribute to Tsodilo's outstanding state of preservation: its remoteness, its low population density, and the high degree of resistance to erosion of its quartzitic rock."

Such physical explanations also need to consider the local inhabitants' spiritual values, their integrity, and their practices as the true fundamental forces behind preservation of the rock art and the Hills. Low population density means little; even a single person can and does deface or pollute a site to make it worthless.

Fig. 11.2 (left):
Photograph taken by Richard Snailman and published in the Sunday Observer newspaper, 6 May 1990. Graffiti scrawled over the Van der Post Panel (**fig. 13.1**) and later removed by the National Museum.

Fig. 11.1 (preceding page):
The site museum. Here, visitors book in to visit the Monument, arrange for guides, and learn about the Hills. The main camping ground lies about one hundred meters to the west. There are ablution blocks, toilets, and trash disposal.

Fig. 11.3 (right):
Names carved into a baobab on the Rhino Trail. Once one person has carved a name, others automatically follow suit.

Fig. 11.4 (above):
The lion painting that gave its name to the Lion Trail. Painted about five meters above ground and on a north-eastern spur of Male Hill,
the lion gazes down the valley that separates Male and Female Hills. Note the geometric designs above and below the lion.

To the pithy dictum "If it pays, it stays" we must add that "if it's used and venerated, it's conserved." Tsodilo has been venerated by different peoples, for different reasons, at different times; conservation management has co-evolved right alongside them.

History of Management

The first managers and conservators of rock art were those who created it. They obviously enjoyed the art, derived meaning from it, restored it, and (even though rare at Tsodilo) sometimes superimposed their contemporary works over art that either was outdated, was unwanted, was diminishing, needed strengthening, or was unknown. The progenitors' management system did not vanish with their demise; it was passed on from generation to generation by word of mouth and practice, and much is kept alive even today. We find evidence in local creation stories, taboos, and veneration of the ancestors (the San) or God (some Hambukushu) as authors of the art. Conservation stems from respect for powers beyond themselves, spiritual powers that, though invisible, are active and invincible.

Into this traditional, effective form of conservation, the National Museum tried to weave the first threads of modern management. Pressures mounted from within and without Tsodilo as tourism rocketed, global interest grew, residents' traditions changed, and the government responded. The resulting Tsodilo Hills Heritage Management Plan called for controlled development and compensation to residents for loss of freedom that still allowed them to develop their village, more or less, without restraint.

Fig. 11.5 (left) & 11.6 (above): Painting of zebra at north end of Female Hill that became the first logo of the National Museum and Art Gallery.

The plan emphasized that "Tsodilo is foremost a heritage area and only secondly a settlement. Thus maintenance of a heritage area must always take precedence over development of the settlement." Under that umbrella the comprehensive plan made specific recommendations for development and maintenance of campsites, staff houses, the site museum, an airstrip, sign boards, brochures, access roads, trails, even research activities. One strength of the plan was that it identified water as a critical need that the National Museum must address as part of the compensation for relocation at the Hills. One weakness was that it focused exclusively on the core area, with no real integration into the wider area beyond the Hills.

The Tsodilo Site Museum

The first and most obvious infrastructure development at Tsodilo was the site museum. Built under thatched roofs at the base of the Hills, and taking its light brown color from the multiple colors of the cliffs, the museum earns its presence in an aesthetically and archaeologically sensitive area **(fig. 11.1)**.

One permanent exhibition, "Welcome to Tsodilo," introduces the visitor to all the physical, natural, and cultural heritage of the site: the vegetation, the cliffs, the rock art in its varieties of red and white paintings, the engravings, the types of archaeological artifacts uncovered during excavations, and a few ethnographic collections of artifacts from the region. A time chart traces inhabitants here from the Stone Age through the Iron Age to the present. The second exhibition, "My Tsodilo," includes local stories on the mythical origins and genesis of the landscape, as well as impressions from more recent researchers and visitors, from Laurens van der Post to some authors of this book. From here, tours into Tsodilo depart for the Hills, led by trained guides, and include helpful brochures and literature.

Fig. 11.7 (above):
Members from a number of southern African countries attending a Southern African Rock Art Project (SARAP) course held at Tsodilo to help administrators and rock art managers work towards seeing major rock art sites in their countries nominated for World Heritage status. Phillip Segadika is seated at the left of the group and Grace Babutsi wearing a cap is standing at the right.

Managing Research

Numerous expeditions have brought spade and brush to Tsodilo, with less ethnological, botanical, and geological research. Botswana's National Museum manages research, with permits granted by the Ministry of Labour and Home Affairs. Illegal excavations are rare, though in September 2004 a foreign tourist and treasure hunter was arrested and fined by a court.

All plans worry about the state of conservation of the rock art, and urge systematic condition surveys every twenty years. The last comprehensive survey, in 1993, took at least three photos of each painting—its entire panel and contextual landscape—and documented the painting's condition. Veld fires continue to be the main threat to Tsodilo, although firebreaks have kept flame and smoke away from the rocks and paintings.

Managing the Intangible

A place may earn UNESCO World Heritage status if it is "directly or tangibly associated with events or living traditions, with ideas, or with beliefs, with artistic and literary works of outstanding universal significance." Tsodilo qualified on several counts: immaculately crafted rock paintings and carvings, occupation spanning the Stone and Metal Ages, continuity of cultural and spiritual affinity to the Hills by people to this day. Yet while it's easy to monitor rock art and physical resources, how does one manage something so nebulous as "heritage"?

The National Museum recognizes the residents' reverence for the Hills as a critical yet vulnerable fabric; a fabric interwoven with threads of ownership, access, privacy, relations, and perceptions; a fabric that must absorb the modern shock waves of tourists, missionaries, scholars, and even HIV/AIDS.

For example, the Juc'hoan headman, who is also a guide, honorary officer of monuments, and member of the task force on management plan review, converted to Christianity. That personal decision has wide and deep implications for intangible heritage at Tsodilo. He may consider certain traditional cultural and ritual practices to be un-Christian, even diabolical, and so end, diminish, or alter a whole set of practices. Likewise, Headman Samutjau Mukate's age and blindness deter him from practicing the divining art for which he was renowned, a skill that has not been passed on to his children or close relations.

Because Tsodilo's culture and belief systems are dynamic, managers must not only adapt to changing realities on the ground, but must also identify the new factors that sustain ownership and usage of intangible heritage. Christian groups now frequent Tsodilo for worship; one particular church dominates the Hills. Perhaps, it is more than coincidence that the final letter "s" on the gate inscription was mysteriously removed, so that new arrivals must now be welcomed to "Tsodilo: The Mountain of the God[ ]"? Does this incident suggest a quiet, invisible ideological battlefield, a subtle shift in political power, or just an accident? What, if anything, should site managers do about the deafening silence of the indigenous belief system? Will replacing the missing "s" spark retaliation and escalate tensions?

The National Musem undertook three projects to strengthen ownership and maintain the relevance of intangible heritage. First, the annual Visual and Performing Arts Festival in Gaborone was extended to Tsodilo; local communities share stories, songs, and dances that venerate the Hills. Second, in 2003 we took GPS coordinates and pictures at landscape features tied to stories and myths in order to encourage guides to celebrate the mysteries behind Tsodilo, how they were named, where sex was born, and how cattle or eland were lowered from the sky by "Karunga" the Almighty. Third, in January 2004 the Minister of Labour and Home Affairs officially recognized Samutjau and C'untae Gcau as honorary officers under the Monuments and Relics Act, at last honoring the traditional leaders for steering the immaculate state of preservation at Tsodilo.

Toward an Integrated Management Plan

In December 2001 UNESCO enshrined Tsodilo on its World Heritage List, praising its intangible heritage and outstanding universal value as "a masterpiece of human creative genius" whose sites bear "a unique or at least exceptional testimony to a cultural tradition or civilization which is living or has disappeared." Yet the praise came with a few conditional strings attached: Tsodilo had to draft a new, integrated management plan, "including an annual schedule of works to be implemented."

Changes since inception of the 1994 draft plan range from museum and staff housing to fences and boreholes to an improved access road that cuts the forty-kilometer journey from Ncamasere from two hours by four-wheel-drive vehicles to thirty minutes by any car. These changes, coupled with World Heritage status, both absorbed and accelerated the flow of visitors, from 2,300 in 2001 to over 10,000 in 2005.

Compounding the pressure, private individuals and companies inundated Tsodilo with requests to develop tourism infrastructure. A new integrated management plan would have to protect the integrity and authenticity of the Tsodilo heritage resources while ensuring enhanced community benefits, both in the core and in the buffer areas (map 11.1).

By June 2005, after almost six months of further research and consultations with the community, the Integrated Management Plan emerged. It zones five main areas, for agriculture, settlement, cattle and wildlife, and low- and high-sensitivity tourism. In such zoning lies its strength.

First, it removes pressure from the Hills; only day visitors can enter the core area, with campsites, lodges, and other developments restricted to outside it. Second, the buffer area helps community tourism development projects. Third, the plan reintroduces wildlife to diversify and enrich the options and experience, drawing more tourists, lengthening their stay, and reducing their pressure on rock paintings alone. Last, it shows how to integrate

Fig. 11.8 (left):
By 1980, tourist numbers were increasing. The Botswana Society, based in Gaborone, took 28 members to visit Tsodilo. A group studies the Rhino Panel on Female Hill at a time before a tourist destroyed the white paintings thinking they were graffiti.

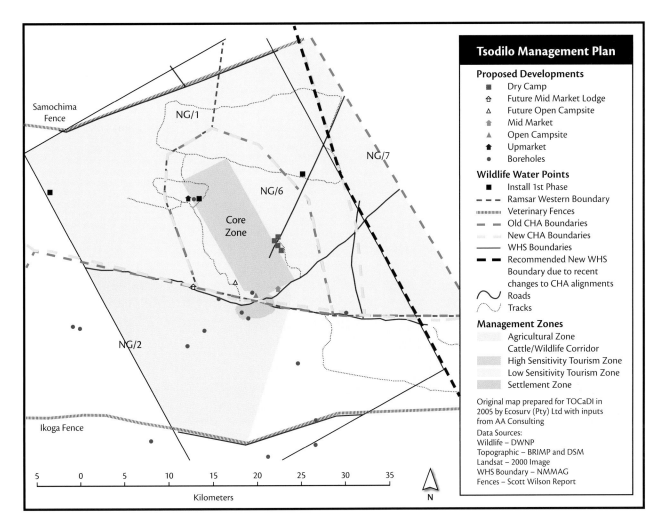

Map 11.1 *(above)*:
Zoning of the Tsodilo Core and Buffer Areas.

administrative machinery for sustainable management throughout the zones. No wonder the plan won the support of both government and critical stakeholders. It promises to be the first of its kind in the nation's management of cultural heritage resources, and it is definitely one of the most vigorous community development schemes for World Heritage Sites in Africa, or indeed, worldwide.

Conclusion

The time, effort, and funds invested in Tsodilo's cultural heritage dwarf those of all of Botswana's other sites combined. Controversial decisions to fence or relocate left a bitter taste for some, but the Integrated Management Plan offers hope for the communities, and could reverse the negatives of past relations. It's clearly a good start that the plan brought permanent employment for ten people from Tsodilo's community, plus opportunities for dozens more who earn hard cash as part-time guides, casual laborers, or craftspeople.

Yet the plan, once fully implemented, could go even further, through arguably the boldest government decisions so far toward rural development and community empowerment. Only a fraction of gate entry fees will go to the National Museum, while the Community Trust will manage, and profit from, every other tourism activity. As it has for millennia, the spiritual, economic, and political life of the Tsodilo Hills may once again be managed of its people, by its people, and for its people. ■

CHAPTER 12

Departing the Hills:
What Stays with You

James G. Workman

There may be several ways to approach the Hills, but whether you arrived on foot, in a vehicle, by airplane, or through the pages of this book, we may all emerge from the Tsodilo experience transformed.

The assumptions you carried here, along with your gear and camera, are no longer quite the same. They have had to adjust, adapt, and widen. The rock art you have imagined, heard about, or seen in photographs appears different when viewed face to face. Perhaps two thousand years old, the paintings seem somehow to live. Even if the meaning isn't crystal clear, you appreciate the choices, techniques, and places where the ancient artists made their canvas of stone. You may have been surprised to see that, while there is no single concentration, the sum total of all the rock art at Tsodilo—hundreds of locations that include more than four thousand paintings—adds up to a multitudinous collection that must be preserved. And now you can see the art as part of a broader context, an integral part to be sure, but inseparable from the Hills and their inhabitants.

What you may not have heard before coming here was how, for many decades, the most valuable "canvas" for "art" was not rock, or ostrich eggshells, but the human body itself. The glittering "paint" additive of choice, specularite, was so highly valued that it was enough to drive men and women to crack and tear apart the walls of the mountains with stone tools and fire in order to get it. The effort required boggles the mind. Tons and tons of rock ore were split open and shattered to extract miniscule quantities of specularite, and the complexity of the operation involved specialized labor and a regional transport and trade network. The mining intensity may also have exhausted the surrounding resources, like trees and water, that could have helped lead to a collapse of the society as the climate grew drier—a cautionary tale for today's equally mining-dependent, resource-intensive industrial economies of southern Africa.

In the last few decades, "mining" of a different, more delicate, and more sustainable kind took place at Tsodilo, and the ore that was extracted and processed may prove more priceless than any minerals. Teams of

Fig. 12.1 (preceding page): Looking across the prehistoric lakebed with Male Hill in the background.

Fig. 12.2 (right): Over five meters up a wall of a shallow shelter on Cliff Trail are images of a striped zebra with lowered head, the silhouette of an eland, other animals, and faded geometric designs.

archaeologists used hand trowels, sieves, brushes, picks, and even tweezers to probe deeper and deeper into the earth. You can imagine their excitement as they peeled back layer after layer of time and sorted, classified, dated, and analyzed these treasures:

- Beads from the Indian Ocean
- Glass from Portugal
- Artificial depressions that may be symbolic
- A child buried in a sitting position facing in a specific direction
- Remnants of a fire that preserved a medieval home's jewelry and tools
- Signs that this place was inhabited ninety to one hundred thousand years ago
- Paintings of cattle, and men on horseback
- And … fish bones, here in the desert

Yes, fish in the desert. While the work may seem tedious and monotonous on some days, it is unexpected discoveries like these that make it so worthwhile. A journal entry dated 11 August 1991, by Mike Murphy, one of the archaeologists, gives a flavor of the camaraderie and routine on a successful working day:

> Again we arose at 6:30 A.M. and had a quick breakfast and I purified some water before we left for the site. We hit an incredible midden of fish bone and other mammal bone along with tools. Alec found a beautiful bone point i.e. fish spear which we all got excited about. It came out of the pit that I was digging. We also found a neat grinding stone probably used to prepare paint as it still had some red pigment on it.
>
> We were quite excited about the fish midden. It was more bone than I've ever seen and we are more than 15 miles from water at the present time. The climate must have been much more wet or some folks walked a long way to get some fish. It took a long time to pick the screens and literally fill bags of material.
>
> Julian and Niall took me up to the top of the rock shelter and we looked over. It was a tough climb but very exciting. I forgot my camera but you could see a great view of the Bushman village and the airstrip. I plan on going back up to take pictures soon.
>
> Later in the day we began to go deep on several holes under the drip-line (the area protected by the rock overhang). Lunch consisted of apples and oranges and corn beef. We were all so dirty. Then back to camp for a warm beer and a climb up to the well for a bath and another beer. Then down to camp for some dinner and Alec got out some Bailey's Irish Crème (to celebrate the discoveries). I helped with dishes and then headed for the sack to write some letters and wrote in my journal.

Archaeology often is filled with such surprises and new discoveries (and warm beer, rather than cold). At White Paintings Shelter the uncovering of levels containing hundreds of fish bones and the discovery of barbed bone fish spears similar to those found hundreds of kilometers to the north in East Africa were big surprises. Alec Campbell found the first barbed point in the sieve in excavation Square 13, between 80 and 90 centimeters below the ground surface.

The well Murphy refers to is of great local importance as a source of water (see page 27). During a dry period, the men discovered that the locally famous well was actually an ancient specularite mine that had partially filled with water after the mining had ceased, a discovery that comes through returning repeatedly and noticing differences. The lower water level revealed a vein of specularite along the wall of the mine. The site is now known as Water Hole Mine. During one field season, the men hauled the "bath" water up from the well each evening in buckets and skimmed off the bird feathers and monkey excrement. They later found out that the well was also the home of a python, and leopards also occasionally drank from it. There were also hundreds of bees attracted by the water and they would sometimes get trapped in towels or clothes. Nonetheless, a bath high up on the side of Tsodilo, coupled with the magnificent view of kudu moving by in the distance as the sun set, appeared to have been worth the risk of periodic bee stings.

The enigmas of rock carving depressions spur the imagination: were they designed to catch the light, form a sphere, or make a sound? The impossibly small adult handprints high on a rock next to an eland: what could they mean? Who removed the "s" from "Gods" at the entrance gate, and why, and how should managers respond? What languages did the farmers, miners, hunters, and gatherers all speak to one another millennia ago, allowing them to live in such proximity for as long as they did? And why did some groups vanish?

Not all of the queries raised on our journeys to Tsodilo have been answered. Perhaps some never can be. But the Hills compel us to ask questions, to look closer, to linger a bit longer, to bounce ideas off our traveling companions and off the rocks and, above all, off our guides, including those living descendants, the Juc'hoansi and the Hambukushu, who still inhabit the landscape.

These families, these communities—they, too, alter our perceptions and leave us transformed. We find they are not now, nor have they ever been, a "primitive" people locked in time, suspended in amber. Their society is dynamic and adapts quickly to changing environmental circumstances, whether of climate, trade, opportunities, or conflict. They never were at all entirely isolated from the subcontinent and they have similar intrinsic human wants and desires and hopes for their children and grandchildren to those of any four-wheel-driving "outsiders."

So for every probing question we ask of them, it should come as no surprise that they have one or two to ask us in return, as fellow families searching for better understanding about our place in the modern world. We may choose to barter with them, or use their services as guides and interpreters, or draw on their stories, passed down through generations. But when tourists exchange currency or goods or handshakes or smiles, however tentative or awkward, they can now do so with the knowledge that they are merely part of a long economic trade tradition that goes back centuries and extended to both of Africa's oceans. Tsodilo's inhabitants, and Tsodilo's outsiders, are all still evolving day by day—and evolving together, interdependently.

Fig. 12.3 (above):
This small painted panel on the Rhino Trail
includes a cow, fish, leaping antelope, and
an indeterminate animal or bird.

Fig. 12.4 (right):
Some sites are located in places difficult to access.
Tourists seated beside a small panel of paintings
—rhino and cattle—in a cliff alcove.

These transforming experiences and memories are what we take away with us when we depart the Hills. We are not the same people we were when we arrived. Perhaps we underestimated the aridity, and grew parched during a hike upon the plateau; this made us appreciate the value of knowing where the hidden seepages were or the shallow lake and slow rivers that once flowed here, before evaporating. Or maybe you climbed Male Hill, gazed out across the Kalahari, and decided that Columbus was wrong, for the world appears flat in every direction as far as the eye can see.

Even beyond our loyalty to the conservation wilderness code that we "leave only footprints and take only photographs," something else stays with us that we can't shake loose. Something about the place lingers: the smell of wood smoke; the sound of the wind at dusk; the stars at night; the songbirds at dawn; the feel of the last undulating sand surface beneath us as we return to the hard paved road; the taste of the dust as we peel off our camp clothing at home. Something remains unexplained. Some spark glowing at the back of our minds or at the belly of our spirits continues to haunt us, inspire us, make us long to return once again, and again, to better understand who, deep down, we really are. ■

FURTHER READINGS

Rock Shelter Archaeology

Brook, G. A., L. H. Robbins, and A. C. Campbell. 2003. Forty thousand years of environmental change in the Kalahari as evidenced by sediments in the Depression Rock Shelter, Tsodilo Hills, Botswana. *Nyame Akuma, Bulletin of the Society of Africanist Archaeologists* 59:2–10.

Robbins, L. H., M. L. Murphy, G. A. Brook, A. H. Ivester, A. C. Campbell, R. G. Klein, R. G. Milo, K. M. Stewart, W. S. Downey, and N. J. Stevens. 2000. Archaeology, palaeoenvironment, and chronology of the Tsodilo Hills White Paintings Rock Shelter, northwest Kalahari Desert, Botswana. *Journal of Archaeological Science* 27:1085–1113.

Robbins, L. H., G. A. Brook, M. L. Murphy, A. C. Campbell, N. Melear, and W. S. Downey. 2000. Late Quarternary archaeological and palaeo-environmental data from sediments at Rhino Cave, Tsodilo Hills, Botswana. *Southern African Field Archaeology* 9:17–31.

Cupules and Grooves

Bednarik, R. G. 1993. Cupules – The oldest surviving rock art. http://mc2.vicnet.net.au/home/cognit/shared_files/cupules

Grossman, L., and N. Goren-Inbar. 2007. Taming rocks and changing landscapes: A new interpretation of neolithic cupmarks. *Current Anthropology* 48 (5):732–40.

Walker, N. 2008. Through the crystal ball: Making sense of spheroids in the Middle Stone Age. *South African Archaeological Bulletin* 63 (187):12–17.

Early Villages and Metalworking

Denbow, J. 1990. Congo to Kalahari: Data and hypotheses about the political economy of the western stream of the Early Iron Age. *African Archaeological Review* 8:139–76.

Denbow, J., and E. Wilmsen. 1986. The advent and course of pastoralism in the Kalahari. *Science* 234:1509–15.

Miller, Duncan. 1996. *The Tsodilo jewelry: Metalwork from northern Botswana.* Cape Town: University of Cape Town Press.

Wilmsen, E. N. 1989. *Land filled with flies: A political economy of the Kalahari.* Chicago: University of Chicago Press.

Specularite Mining

Beaumont, P. B. 1973. The ancient pigment mines of southern Africa. *South African Journal of Science* 69:140–46.

Robbins, L. H., M. L. Murphy, A. C. Campbell, and G. A. Brook. 1998. Intensive mining of specular hematite in the Kalahari ca. AD 800–1000. *Current Anthropology* 39:144–50.

Rock Art

Campbell, A. C., J. Denbow, and E. Wilmsen. 1994. Paintings like engravings: Rock art at Tsodilo. In *Contested images: Diversity in southern African rock art research*, ed. T. A. Dowson and D. Lewis-Williams, 131–59. Johannesburg: Witwatersrand University Press.

Fig. 13.1 (preceding page):
Four members of the Juc'hoansi village approaching the Van der Post Panel.

Smith, B. W., and S. Ouzman. 2004. Taking stock: Identifying Khoekhoen herder rock art in southern Africa. *Current Anthropology* 45 (4):499–526.

The South African Museum of Rock Art. 2007. *Thread of knowledge – Tracing the meaning of southern African rock art. An educator's resource book.* Johannesburg: Rock Art Research Institute.

General Readings on the Archaeology of Southern Africa and Botswana

Lane, P. A. Reid, and A. Segobye. 1998. *Ditswa mmung: The archaeology of Botswana.* Gaborone, Botswana: The Botswana Society, Pula Press.

Mitchell, P. 2002. *The archaeology of southern Africa.* Cambridge: Cambridge University Press.

Reid, A. 2005. Interaction, marginalization and the archaeology of the Kalahari. Chapter 14 in *African archaeology*, ed. A. B. Stahl. Malden, Mass.: Blackwell Publishing.

San

Barnard, A. 1992. *Hunters and herders of southern Africa.* Cambridge: Cambridge University Press.

Biesele, M. 1974. A note on the beliefs of modern Bushmen concerning the Tsodilo Hills (paintings). *Newsletter of the Southwest African Scientific Society* 15 (3-4):1–3.

Hitchcock, R. K., K. Ikeya, M. Biesele, and R. B. Lee, eds. 2006. *Updating the San: image and reality of an African people in the 21st century.* Senri Ethnological Studies no. 70, National Museum of Ethnology, Osaka, Japan.

Lee, R. B. 1979. *The !Kung San: Men, women and work in a foraging society.* Cambridge: Cambridge University Press.

Hambukushu

Larson, T. J. 1972. *Tales from the Okavango.* Cape Town: Howard Timmins.

———. 2001. *Dibete of the Okavango.* New York: Writers Club Press.

———. 2001. *Hambukushu – Rainmakers of the Okavango.* New York: Writers Club Press.

Passarge, S. *Quellen zur Khoisan – Forschung.* Pages 285 to 304 in *The Kalahari ethnographies (1896-1898) of Siegfried Passarge*, ed. E. Wilmsen, 1997 Cologne: Rüdiger Köppe Verlag.

The Environment, Present and Past

Hargreaves, B. J. 2007. *Important plants of Tsodilo.* Ed. P. Hargreaves. Gaborone, Botswana: National Museum, Monuments and Art Gallery.

Thomas, D. S. G., and P. A. Shaw. 1991. *The Kalahari environment.* Cambridge: Cambridge University Press.

Thomas, D. S. G., G. Brook, P. A. Shaw, M. Bateman, K. Haberyan, C. Appleton, D. Nash, S. McLaren, and F. Davies. 2003. Late Pleistocene wetting and drying in the NW Kalahari: An integrated study from the Tsodilo Hills, Botswana. *Quaternary International* 1041:53–67.

Travel and History

Van der Post, L. 1998. *The lost world of the Kalahari.* Illustrated by David Coulson. London: Chatto and Windus. (Orig. pub. 1958.)

Wilmsen, E., ed. 1997. *The Kalahari ethnographies (1896-1898) of Siegfried Passarge: Nineteenth century Khoisan- and Bantu-speaking peoples.* Cologne: Rüdiger Köppe Verlag.

ABOUT THE AUTHORS

ABOUT THE AUTHORS

Grace Babutsi is a senior technical officer of archaeological collections and documentation at the Botswana National Museum in Gaborone. She has worked with many archaeological researchers in Botswana with special emphasis on the Tsodilo Hills, Bosutswe, and Toteng.

George A. Brook is the Merle Prunty Professor of Geography at the University of Georgia and is also Director of the Luminescence Dating Laboratory. He has B.S., M.S., and Ph.D. degrees from Edinburgh, Witwatersrand, and McMaster University. His research focuses on relationships between Quaternary environmental change and human populations in southern Africa, Belize, and Argentina, and he also conducts paleoclimate research in China and Egypt.

Alexander (Alec) Colin Campbell was born in England and has a B.A. from Rhodes University, South Africa. He has lived in Botswana since 1962. He served as Director of the Department of Wildlife and National Parks in Botswana and initiated the National Museum and Art Gallery (now the Botswana National Museum) in 1966. He retired as its Director in 1987. Most recently he was a founding director of the Trust for African Rock Art, Nairobi, and has recorded rock art in sixteen African countries, including much of the Sahara.

James R. Denbow is an associate professor of archaeology and anthropology at the University of Texas at Austin. He earned his B.A. in anthropology at the University of Illinois, Urbana. He received his M.A. and Ph.D. in anthropology and African studies from Indiana University in Bloomington. He established and ran the antiquities program at the National Museum of Botswana between 1979 and 1986, and has also conducted archaeological research in the Republic of Congo and Malawi. He has ongoing archaeological projects in the Kalahari and has published two books and many articles and reports on that region.

Robert K. Hitchcock is a professor and Chair of the Department of Anthropology at Michigan State University. He has worked with San peoples in Botswana, Namibia, and Zimbabwe for the past thirty years, as well as with indigenous peoples elsewhere in Africa and in the United States, Guatemala, Peru, and Canada. At present, Dr. Hitchcock is working with African refugees in the United States as well as with American Indians involved in natural resource management and cultural heritage programs. He is a member of the board and past co-president of the Kalahari Peoples Fund, an advocacy and development organization that provides assistance to San, Nama, and other peoples of southern Africa.

Fig. 14.1 (preceding page):
Cliffs along the west side of Female Hill. Note the hyena seated on the right of the dark tree trunk in middle foreground.

Michael (Mike) L. Murphy (B.S., Grand Valley State University, M.A., Western Michigan University, Ph.D. in anthropology, Michigan State University, 1999) is an anthropology instructor at Kalamazoo Valley Community College and Kellogg Community College in Michigan. He has conducted archaeological research at Tsodilo Hills and other sites in Botswana, and also in Michigan. In addition, he has worked on an archaeological project in Mexico. Dr. Murphy is a stone tool specialist who has excavated and analyzed artifacts from the Middle Stone Age and early part of the Later Stone Age at White Paintings Shelter.

Lawrence (Larry) H. Robbins (B.A., M.A., University of Michigan, Ph.D. in anthropology from the University of California, Berkeley) is a professor emeritus of anthropology at Michigan State University. He did pioneering archaeological research at Lake Turkana, Kenya, in 1965–66, where he discovered the ancient fishing settlement at Lothagam Hill. He has also worked in the Karamoja area of Uganda. Since 1982 his research has focused on the Tsodilo Hills and other sites in Botswana. Professor Robbins is the author of *Stones, Bones and Ancient Cities*, as well as numerous publications on his research.

Phillip Segadika is a principal curator of the Archaeology and Monuments Division at the Botswana National Museum in Gaborone, Botswana. His interest areas are landscape archaeology research and formulation of management plans.

Michael Taylor (B.Sc, B.soc.Sci [Hons], University of Cape Town, Ph.D. in social anthropology, University of Edinburgh) works for the International Land Coalition in Rome, Italy, an alliance of global and local organizations working to promote equity in access to land and natural resources. He was born and grew up in Botswana. Between 1993 and 2001 he was Assistant Curator of Ethnology at the National Museum, mainly conducting ethnographic and historical research in different areas of Botswana. He then worked for the United Nations Development Programme and Ministry of Agriculture on a natural resource management project in Botswana, Kenya, and Mali, before moving to his present position in 2006.

Edwin N. Wilmsen is a research associate in the Department of Anthropology, University of Texas-Austin and Honorary Fellow of the Centre for African Studies, University of Edinburgh. Since 1973, he has done both archaeological and ethnographic research in Botswana and is the author of *Land Filled with Flies: A Political Economy of the Kalahari* and *Journeys with Flies*, a meditation on his engagement with the peoples of Botswana.

James G. Workman, a Yale and Oxford history graduate, is an award-winning journalist, editor, and speechwriter with a strong focus on water and natural resources. For seven years he lived and worked in southern Africa, writing out of a Land Rover about the causes and consequences of water scarcity. He tracked the ongoing conflict between Botswana and the Bushmen in the Central Kalahari, the basis of his book, *Heart of Dryness: How the Last Bushmen Can Help Us Endure the Coming Age of Permanent Drought*.

ILLUSTRATIONS CREDITS

George A. Brook   **figs. 2.3** (NASA), **2.6, 2.8, 6.4.**

Alec Campbell   **front cover, inside front cover, frontispiece, figs. A.1, A.2, 0.1, 0.2, 0.4, 0.8, 0.12, 1.1, 1.2, 1.3, 1.4, 1.5, 1.7, 1.8, 1.9, 1.10, 1.11, 1.13, 2.1, 2.2, 2.4, 2.5, 2.7, 2.9, 2.10, 2.11, 2.12, 2.13, 2.14, 2.15, 2.16, 2.17, 2.18, 2.19, 2.20, 3.1, 3.2, 3.6, 3.8, 3.9, 3.10, 3.12, 3.16, 3.17, 4.1, 4.2, 4.4, 5.1, 6.1, 6.2, 6.3, 6.6, 6.8, 7.1, 7.2, 7.5, 7.8, 7.15, 7.19, 7.27, 7.28, 8.1, 8.2, 8.3, 8.4, 8.6, 8.7, 9.1, 9.2, 9.4, 10.1, 10.2, 10.3, 10.4, 10.5, 10.6, 10.7, 11.1, 11.3, 11.7, 11.8, 12.1, 12.2, 12.4, 14.1, 16.1, inside back cover.**

David Coulson   **figs. 0.3, 0.5, 0.6, 0.7, 0.11, 3.13, 4.3, 7.16, 7.22, 7.23, 7.24, 7.27, 8.5, 11.5, 13.1.**

James R. Denbow   **figs. 5.11, 5.16c.**

Catherine Guest   **figs. 7.26, 11.4, 15.1.**

Michael Main   **fig. 7.10.**

Mike Murphy   **fig. 9.3.**

Larry Robbins   **figs. 3.3, 3.4, 3.5, 3.7, 3.11, 3.14, 3.15, 3.19, 6.5, 6.7.**

Edwin N. Wilmsen   **figs. 5.2, 5.3, 5.4, 5.5, 5.6, 5.7, 5.8, 5.9, 5.10, 5.12, 5.13, 5.14, 5.15, 5.16a, 5.16b. 5.16d.**

All drawings were prepared by Alec Campbell.

We thank Harry N. Abrams Inc., New York, for permission to republish six of the drawings which originally appeared in *African Rock Art: Paintings and Engravings on Stone* (2001).

The drawing of the Rhino Panel **(fig. 0.10)** is copied from François Balsan, *Capricorn Road*. Philosophical Library Inc., New York (1955).

The pen-and-ink wash by William Burchell **(fig. 6.9)** was redrawn from Plate XI in *The South African Drawings of William J. Burchell* Vol 1. *The Bachapins of Litākun*, edited by Helen M. McKay and published by Witwatersrand University Press, Johannesburg (1938).

The photograph taken by Richard Snailman **(fig. 11.2)** appeared in the *Sunday Observer*, 6 May 1990.

Siegfried Passarge's map of Tsodilo Hills **(map 0.2)** is taken from his book, *Die Kalahahri*. Dietrich Reimer (Ernst Vohsen). Berlin (1904).

Siegfried Passarge's drawing **(fig. 0.9)** is taken from his book, *Die Buschmänner der Kalahahri*. Dietrich Reimer (Ernst Vohsen). Berlin (1907).

MAPS

Notes about this Map

1. Lines defining hills are not contour lines, they reflect levels and provide a general indication of the shape of the Hills.

2. The road from Ncamasere to the Hambukushu Village at Tsodilo has a relatively smooth and hard surface and is suitable for sedan cars. However, as of March 2009, the last four kilometers from the Village to Museum Headquarters are rough and can be muddy during the rainy season.

3. Camping is only allowed in officially designated campsites. There is a large campsite at Museum Headquarters with ablution blocks. Three other smaller campsites offer nothing except cleared areas and trash bins.

4. Trails are marked in red on the map. Rhino and Lion Trails are relatively easy to follow. However, visitors are advised to hire guides who will ensure they see all they wish to see and do not become lost. Certainly, visitors must hire guides if they intend to follow Cliff or Divuyu Trails or to wander off the recognized paths.

   Warning: one stretch each on Rhino and Cliff Trails is fairly steep and requires scrambling over rocks, which can be slippery.

5. The main route to the summit of Male Hill is marked on the map. The climb takes a fit person about one hour with an ascent of 400 meters.

6. Four groups of people have given names to the Hills and places on them. The first to do so were Ncaekhoe who gave the earliest remembered names. The last Ncae man left Tsodilo in the early twentieth century. Juc'hoansi, who began to visit the Hills in about 1850, adopted some Ncae names and gave some places their own names. Hambukushu, who settled soon after 1850, also gave names to the Hills and places on them. Finally, a few places have been given English names since 1960.

Translations of some of the names have been included on page 177.

While this map provides an accurate plan of the Hills, the exact locations of sites have not been indicated with dots.

Fig. 15.1 (right):
Cliffs above Tshokgam, the Python Spring. Compare with **Fig. 0.2** *on page 4 to see how colours on rocks change when bathed in evening light.*

TSODILO HILLS MAP

NORTH HILL

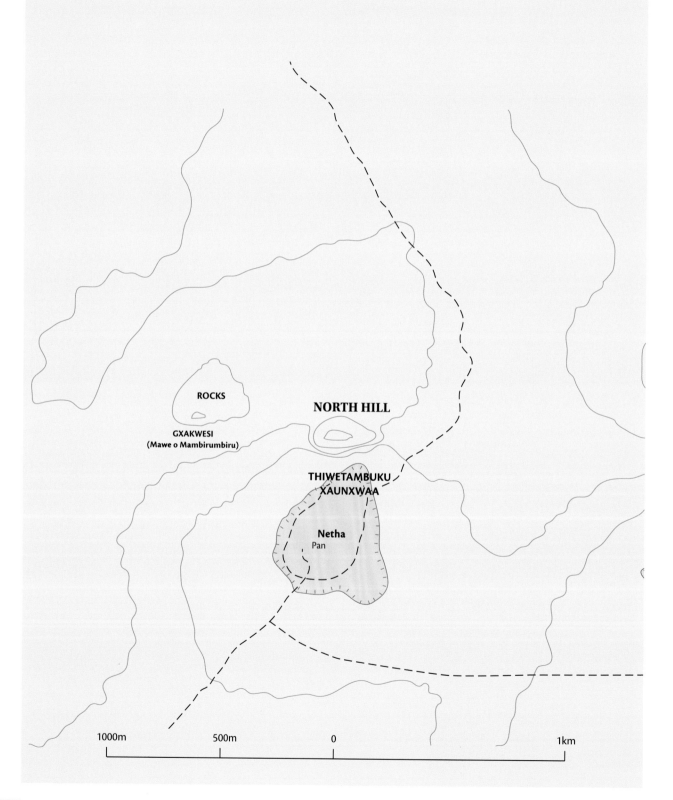

ROCKS

NORTH HILL

GXAKWESI
(Mawe o Mambirumbiru)

THIWETAMBUKU
XAUNXWAA

Netha
Pan

1000m   500m   0   1km

CHILD HILL

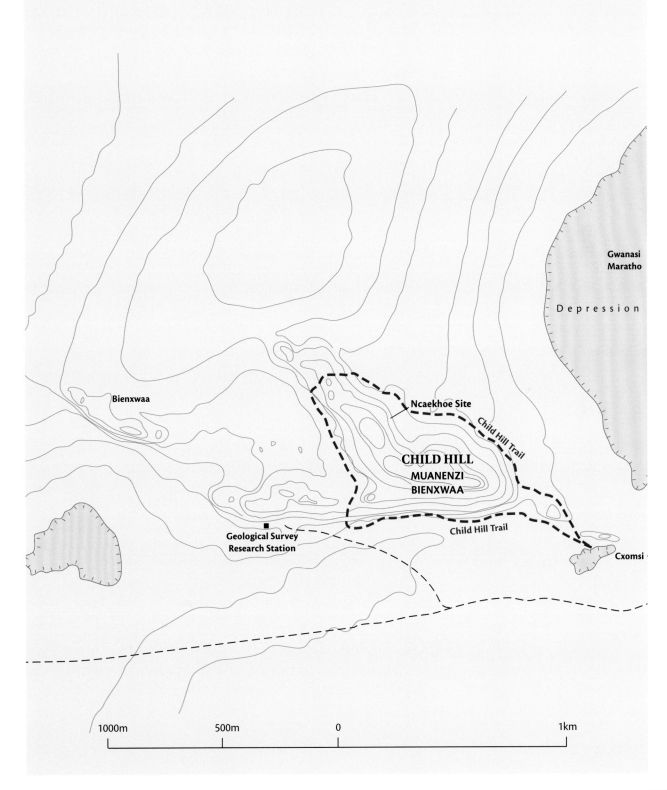

N

Gwanasi
Maratho

Depression

Bienxwaa

Ncaekhoe Site

Child Hill Trail

CHILD HILL
MUANENZI
BIENXWAA

Geological Survey
Research Station

Child Hill Trail

Cxomsi

| 1000m | 500m | 0 | 1km |

FEMALE HILL

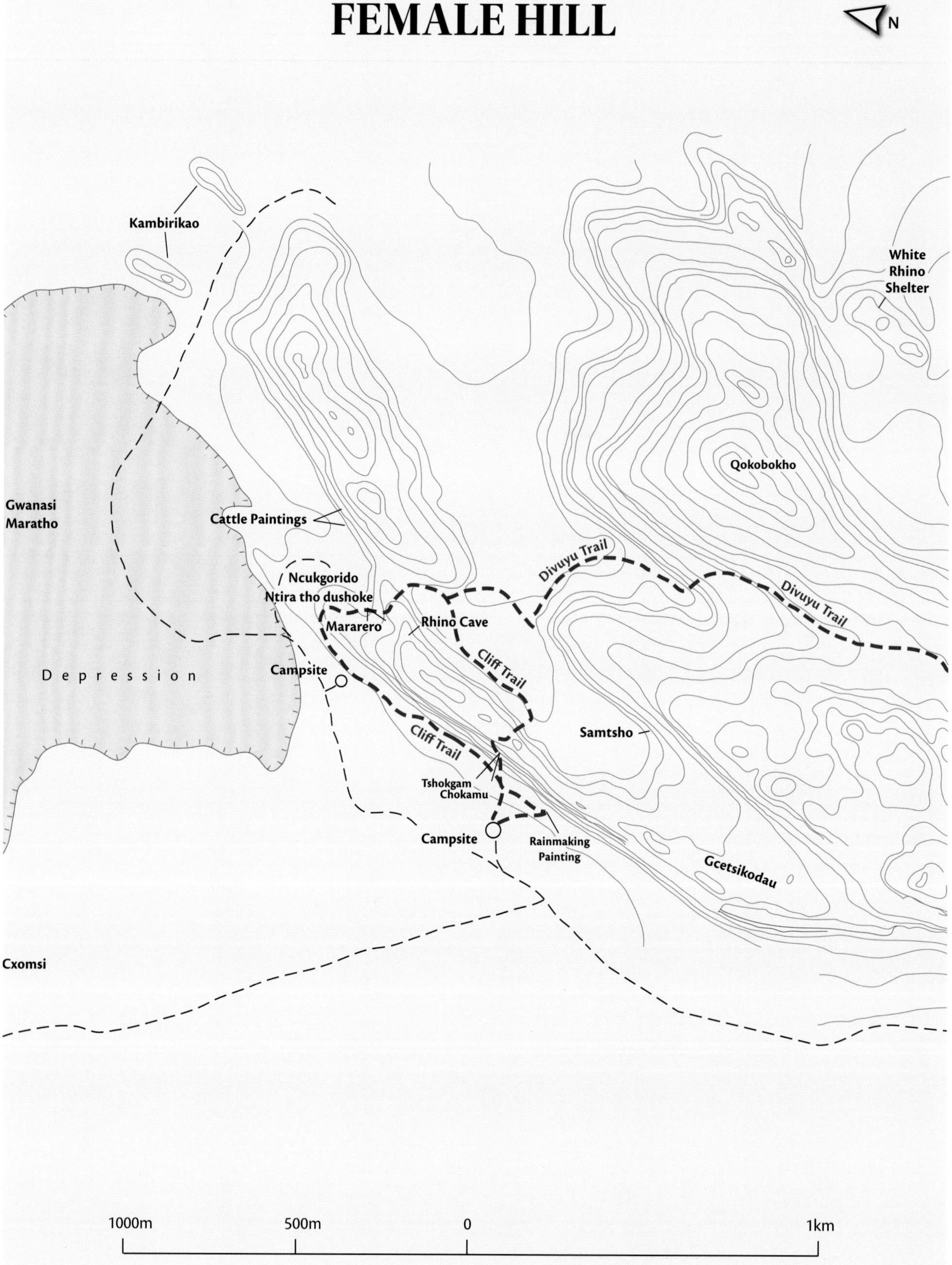

N

Kambirikao

White
Rhino
Shelter

Gwanasi
Maratho

Cattle Paintings

Qokobokho

Ncukgorido
Ntira tho dushoke

Rhino Cave

Divuyu Trail

Divuyu Trail

Mararero

Cliff Trail

Depression

Campsite

Cliff Trail

Samtsho

Tshokgam
Chokamu

Campsite

Rainmaking
Painting

Gcetsikodau

Cxomsi

1000m   500m   0   1km

FEMALE HILL (continued)

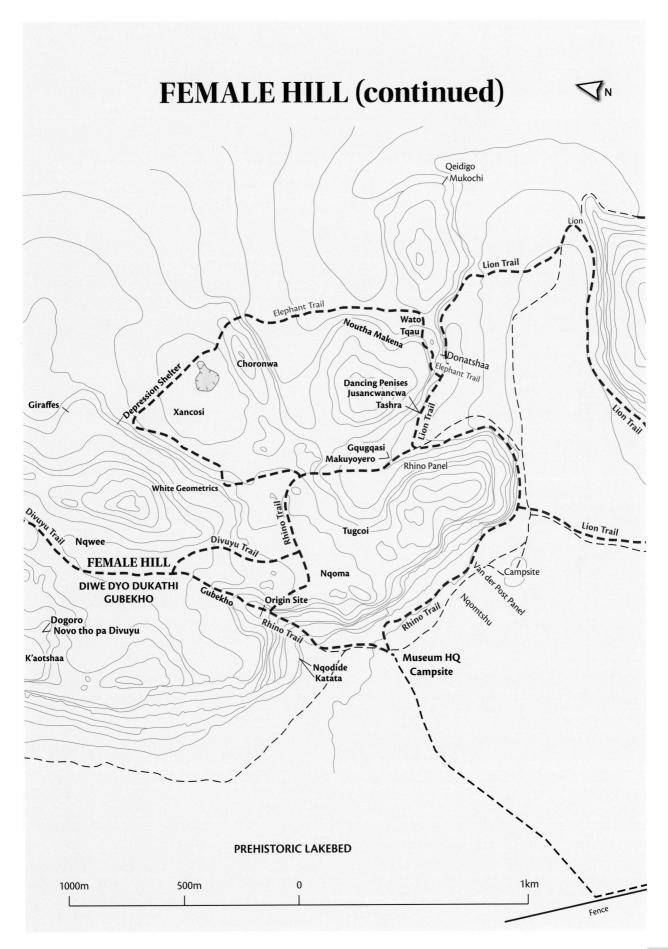

N

Qeidigo
Mukochi

Lion

Lion Trail

Elephant Trail

Noutha Makena

Wato
Tqau

Donatshaa

Elephant Trail

Choronwa

Depression Shelter

Dancing Penises
Jusancwancwa
Tashra

Lion Trail

Giraffes

Xancosi

Gqugqasi
Makuyoyero

Rhino Panel

Lion Trail

White Geometrics

Rhino Trail

Tugcoi

Lion Trail

Divuyu Trail

Nqwee

Divuyu Trail

Nqoma

Van der Post Panel

Campsite

FEMALE HILL

DIWE DYO DUKATHI
GUBEKHO

Gubekho

Origin Site

Rhino Trail

Ngomtshu

Dogoro
Novo tho pa Divuyu

Rhino Trail

Museum HQ
Campsite

K'aotshaa

Nqodide
Katata

PREHISTORIC LAKEBED

1000m   500m   0   1km

Fence

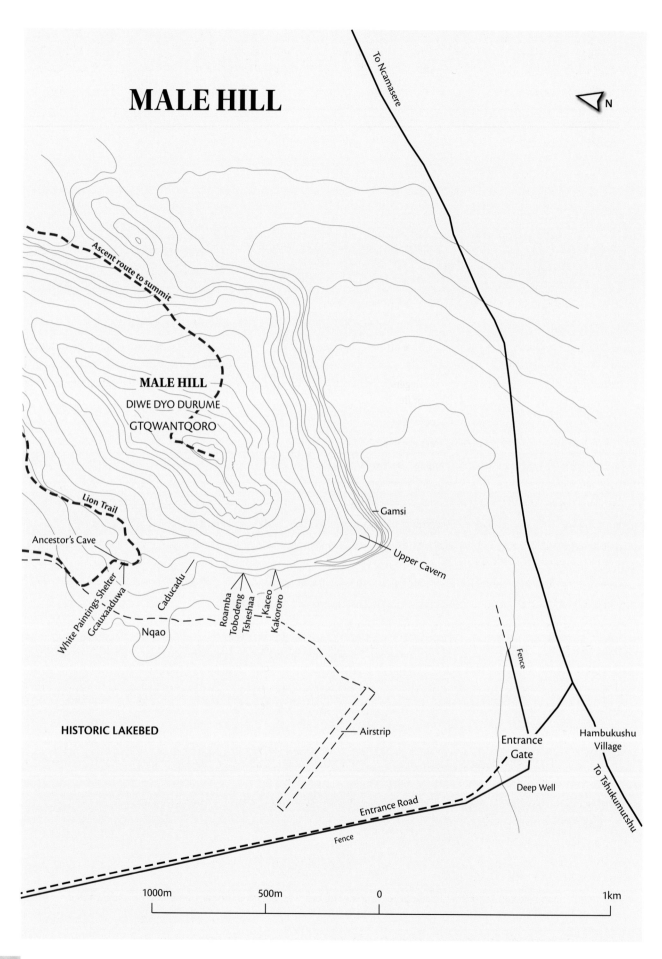

MALE HILL

To Ncamasere

MALE HILL

DIWE DYO DURUME

GTQWANTQORO

Ascent route to summit

Lion Trail

Ancestor's Cave

White Paintings Shelter

Gcauxaaduwa

Nqao

Caducadu

Roamba
Tobodeng
Tsheshaa
Kaceo
Kakororo

Gamsi

Upper Cavern

Fence

HISTORIC LAKEBED

Airstrip

Entrance
Gate

Hambukushu
Village

To Tshukumutshu

Deep Well

Entrance Road

Fence

1000m   500m   0   1km

TRANSLATION OF NAMES OF THE TSODILO HILLS

According to the residents of the Hills, they were told by the original Ncae inhabitants (who left the Hills in the early twentieth century) that in the beginning the Hills were people. The Male had two wives, and they lived next to him. However, the Male liked the large Female more than the other—this was his second wife. She stayed next to him, as the Female Hill. The first wife became jealous and ran away, past the Child Hill, who was not married. She wanted to keep on running, but the others sent their servants to stop her, and she remained where she is (North Hill).

The names of the Hills are found in four different languages. Many of the names are from the original Ncae inhabitants. Others are in Juc'hoan, and yet others in Mbukushu, the languages of the current residents of the Hills. The names, now, have also been translated into English.

Caducadu (Juc'hoan): drip-drip. This is a gap in the rock that had water in it after rains. In order to get water, one had to stick a small bunch of grass in the crack, and then suck the water droplets off the grass.

Divuyu (Mbukushu): baobab tree.

Dogoro (Ncae): small anthills. Named after the many anthills in the area. This was a favourite living spot in the past, and kudu often used to shelter in the nearby cave when it was cold.

Gcaoxaduwa (Ncae): shelter of the buffalos. This is where Ncae used to store buffalo meat after successful hunts.

Gwanasi (Juc'hoan): salt lick. Wild animals were often found here, attracted by the salt at the bottom of the pan. Mbukushu call it '*Maratho*' which has the same meaning.

Gxakwesi (Juc'hoan): servants. According to legend these are the servants of the group of Hills that went to block the path of *Xaunxwaa* (North Hill) so that she would not flee further.

Jusancwancwa (Juc'hoan): 'The naked people.' Dancing Penises Shelter.

Katata (Mbukushu): rock fig. These fig trees are plentiful in this gorge.

Kaceo (Juc'hoan): pond. A small spring appears here when it rains.

Makuyoyero (Mbukushu): the place of washing. This place used to be a site of perennial water and their ancestors would wash here. Now the water is deep underground. Ncae called this site '*Gqugqasi*' meaning 'where the water soaks into the ground.'

Ncukgoridau (Ncae): the path of sex. According to legend, this was the site where people first had sex.

Nduthamakena (Mbukushu): Makena's house. Makena was the name of an Mbukushu woman who was born in the cave when her parents were staying at the Hills.

Gamsi (Ncae): Place of the lions. Lions sometimes used to birth in these caves.

Nqao (Juc'hoan): knobthorn tree. The site of the Juc'hoansi village until the mid-1990s.

Nqomtshu (Juc'hoan): porcupine hole. In the past there was a well here.

Nqwee (Juc'hoan): valley. There are a lot of wild fruit trees in this high valley and it used to be a favourite gathering place.

Popa (Ncae): shelter. This is where their ancestors lived during the rainy season as it provided a shelter.

Qeidiqo (Juc'hoan): mortar (that is used for stamping corn with a pestle). In Mbukushu this place is called '*Mokochi*', named after an Mbukushu man who often relied on this well for water, and whose descendants now live in Shakawe.

Thiwethambuku (Mbukushu): the one who wants to live alone.

Tobodeng (Juc'hoan): jackalberry trunk. There was once a very large jackalberry tree growing here, which has since died. There was also a small spring here that had water after rains. Hambukushu call it '*Kakororo*' meaning 'to scoop out' because water trickled down a small crack in the rocks and could be scooped into a bucket.

Tqau (Ncae): furrow. This place is called '*Wato*' in Mbukushu, meaning 'dugout canoe' because of the shape in the rock.

Tshokgam (Ncae): medicine mouth. This cave was a reliable water source in the past. The cave is, in fact, a prehistoric specularite mine and sometimes known in English as 'Python Spring'.

Tshotshaa (Ncae): medicine water. An important well where water used to trickle from the cliff into a small pool. In Mbukushu it is called '*Roamba*' meaning 'shallow.'

Xancosi (Juc'hoan): old village. This was a favourite camping site as it was near to Gubekho where water could be found.

~ Michael Taylor and Alec Campbell

INDEX

Bold indicates photo, figure, or map.

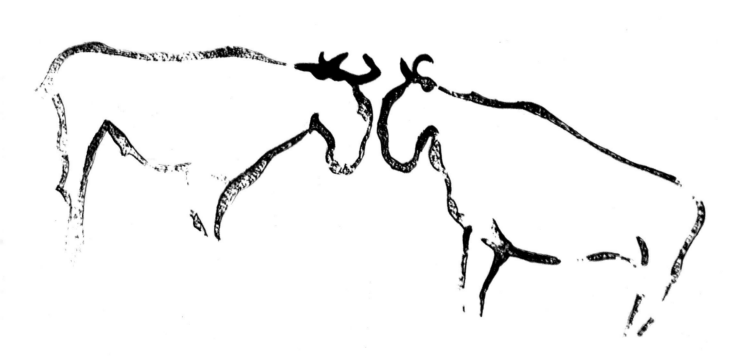

Fig. 16.1 (below):
Wildebeest stand face to face in a cave high above Cliff Trail.